C000203235

COUNTRY
WIDE

COUNTRY
WIDE

**A collection of the best writing by
RTÉ presenter, Damien O'Reilly, from
his weekly *Irish Farmers Journal* columns**

Ballpoint Press

For Deirbhile and Patrick

Published in 2017 by Ballpoint Press
4 Wyndham Park, Bray, Co Wicklow, Republic of Ireland
Telephone: 00353 86 821 7631
Email: ballpointpress1@gmail.com
Web: www.ballpointpress.ie

ISBN 978-0-995479340

© Copyright Damien O'Reilly, 2017

All rights reserved. No part of this publication may be reproduced,
stored in a retrieval system, or in any form or by any means,
without the prior permission in writing of the publisher, nor be
otherwise circulated in any form of binding or cover other than that
in which it is published and without a similar condition including
this condition being imposed on the subsequent publisher.

While every effort has been made to ensure the accuracy of
all information contained in this book, neither the author
nor the publisher accepts liability for any errors or omissions made.

Book design and production by Joe Coyle Media&Design,
joecoyledesign@gmail.com

© Cover photograph by Matthew Thompson for RTÉ Radio 1
Inside photographs courtesy of RTÉ, John Caffrey,
Irish Farmers Journal and Damien O'Reilly's personal collection

Printed and bound by GraphyCems

Contents

Foreword

LIKE so many people in this country Damien O'Reilly would appear to have a split personality! Is he a Dub or a Cavan man? He's certainly not sure and for that matter neither am I.

What I am sure of though is that Damien was probably the only pupil at O'Connell's CBS who spent every weekend lambing ewes, dosing calves or making silage depending on the season.

His description of idyllic childhood summers on his granny's farm in Derrylea surrounded by cousins and neighbours evokes powerful images of community in rural Ireland. His discovery of Gaelic football and the GAA added to this community family.

From the time he was a little boy Damien was a listener. He listened to the stories of his granny Margaret and uncle Philip and to those of the customers in his father's pub.

That not-so-common skill has helped make Damien an award winning broadcaster and journalist. It has given an authenticity to his writing that has won him the trust of the people he writes for and about. It's what made him a natural fit as a columnist for the *Irish Farmers Journal* and our readers. And it's what makes this collection of his columns in the *Farmers Journal* such a joy to read.

Damien continues to listen, broadcast and write and long may he do so.

Mairead Lavery
Editor, Irish Country Living, *Irish Farmers Journal*

Acknowledgements

I WOULD like to thank Mairead Lavery, editor of the *Irish Country Living* for having the faith in me to write a weekly column in the paper. I would also like to thank sub-editor Joe Lenehan for his patience every week including those weeks when I have a last-minute change to make.

I would like to make it clear that the views in these columns and in these pages are my own and not those of RTÉ or the *Irish Farmers Journal*. I have edited and in some cases amended information in the columns for the purpose of bringing them up to date. I have chosen various pieces from the period 2010 to the present.

Thanks also to Ballpoint Press and its designer Joe Coyle for bringing this book together so well.

A big thank you to Tom McGuire, the head of RTÉ Radio 1 and my boss for lending his support to this book. Also to my fantastic friends and work colleagues in the radio centre, thank you. I would also like to acknowledge the support and guidance from two great friends, David Markey and Shay Keany, in piecing this project together.

Finally, I want to thank my family and in particular my two best friends, my children Deirbhile and Patrick who inspire me.

Damien O'Reilly
August 2017

About the Author

DAMIEN O'REILLY has worked for RTÉ since May 1998. He presents *Countrywide*, the popular Saturday morning programme on RTÉ Radio 1.

He was named PPI speech broadcaster of the year in 2015. Back in 1997, Damien won the prestigious McNamee Award presented for excellence in broadcasting by the GAA while working for local radio station Shannonside/Northern Sound.

In 2012 and 2016, he won the International Federation of Agricultural Journalists Star Prize for broadcasting. Damien has produced, presented and reported for a range of well-known RTÉ radio programmes including acting as stand-in presenter on Joe Duffy's *Liveline* and Mary Wilson's *Drivetime* on RTÉ Radio 1. He has also reported for various news and sports programmes.

Since 2010, Damien has written a weekly column entitled 'Damien's Diary' for the *Irish Country Living* section of the *Irish Farmers Journal* newspaper.

He is a founder member and current secretary of the European Network of Agricultural Journalists.

Prologue 1
'I don't want to go back to Dublin'

IT was towards the end of August. A milky sunny Sunday evening. I must have been sitting in the tree overlooking the "big field" for two hours. Alone. Whimpering. It was the end of summer. The field was becoming green again after the second cut of silage a few weeks earlier. I could hear the wind rustling the leaves in the tree, that sort of early autumnal breeze and the shadow of the tree protruding across the big field was longish and skinny. The sun was sickly and pale in the sky. It was around six o clock and beginning to get a bit chilly.

The curtain was coming down after another long, adventure-filled, hot, happy, carefree summer bouncing around the farm, spoiled for money and sweets and Cavan Cola. Some of the bottles spelt Cola with a K as in Kola. It didn't matter. It tasted the same, like no other. It was to me, what a pint of Guinness was to a man drinker. We didn't get Cavan Kola in Dublin. You could only get Cavan Kola in, well, Cavan. No more Cavan Kola. No more days at the silage. No more getting 50p pieces and the odd pound note from visiting neighbours. No more club championship matches in Breffni Park. No more acting the goat with my cousins. No more spoiling from Granny. No more sweets and chocolate from my visiting aunties. No more trips to the mart or sitting in Langtrys pub listening to the seven or eight male farmers talking and talking and talking on a Saturday night. And me among them, drinking my Cavan Kola.

Summer was over. School would recommence. And I was sitting in the tree overlooking the 'big field' in silence. It was like looking out onto Croke Park at around seven o'clock the night of the All Ireland final. Empty. All the fun and colour and happiness over. Seagulls squalling overhead. Dusk looming. Paper wrappers whistling along the stands. As the clock ticked that Sunday evening towards the time when my father would say, "right, well we better head off", I snuck off up the hill field towards the 'big field'.

I didn't want to go home.

I was sick to the pit of my stomach. So I hid. For two long hours. I could hear them all down below at the house shouting my name. "Damien! Damien! Where are you? Come on, we're going home"... home being Castleknock in Dublin.

I was born and bred in Dublin to country parents. Mam is from Kildare. Or is it Offaly? Depends who is doing well in the football! She is from a place exotically called Kishavanna which is on the Kildare side of the Offaly town of Edenderry. Kishavanna is in Carbury. And Carbury is the club of famed Kildare All Star goalkeeper Ollie Crinnigan. My mother was a Crinnigan. Ollie was her cousin. Crinnigan, a most unusual name. When I would meet a Kildare supporter, I say that my mother is from Kildare.

"Where?"

"Carbury."

"What was her name?"

"Pauline Crinnigan"

"Oh anything to Ollie?"

When her school friend Seamus Darby scored that famous goal against Kerry in 1982 to prevent the Kingdom winning the five-in-a-row of All Irelands, I thought she was from Offaly such were the screeches and cheering in our living room. But she has an all-white outfit which she wears too whenever Kildare are up in Croke Park. So a bit like me, she can't decide where she comes from! I cheer for Cavan even though I am from Dublin. That is because Dad is from Cavan. Ballyjamesduff to be precise. And his name is Paddy. Paddy Reilly from Ballyjamesduff. His sisters and brothers call him Pat. So to them he is Pat O'Reilly. When he came to Dublin to work in the sixties, a few liberties were taken by the locals who renamed him Paddy Reilly. And so when we would be all packed into the car heading for Ballyjamesduff to visit Granny on a Sunday, we were made believe, the famous Percy French ballad 'Come Back Paddy Reilly to Ballyjamesduff' playing on the radio was written about him!

He didn't make us any the wiser until we were old enough to work it out for ourselves… us being, my two younger brothers Kenneth and Pauric and the youngest my sister Siobhan. I am the eldest of four. They are true blue Dubs. I am the oddball who shouts against them whenever Cavan play Dublin.

And that is because I spent so much of my childhood on the farm in Ballyjamesduff with my Granny Margaret and my uncle Philip, Dad's older brother, the farmer. For the first four or five years of my life, Christmas Day was spent with the family in my Nana's in Kishavanna. From then until about the age of 18, they were spent with Granny and Philip in Ballyjamesduff. Derrylea, Ballyjamesduff to be precise. On Christmas Day, we would go to have dinner with my Auntie Kathleen, Dad's sister and her husband Michael Clarke in Cavan town. And boy was I spoilt.

Summers, Easter, Halloween, mid-term breaks and any other weekend I could, I spent on the farm. To think now that my own son, Patrick, would be off on his own with relations on Christmas Day makes me laugh. How odd was that? Mam, Dad, Kenneth, Pauric and Siobhan in Castleknock eating their Christmas dinner. And me in Cavan town, 75 miles away happy out! The only downside was I had to wait until they came to visit on St. Stephen's Day to get Santa's present.

But I knew no different. I would go back to school after a stint in Cavan with my chest out. I felt superior after a weekend dosing calves, moving cattle, cleaning the byre, fencing a field, lambing ewes, calving cows, going to the mart, playing football on my own with calf buckets as goals, commentating to myself in the 'white field' and drinking gallons of Cavan Kola. My schoolmates lived a sheltered life compared to my other life in Ballyjamesduff.

And to this day, I know I was right to believe that. I know that those times grounded me out for the career I am in today. I grew up going to Cavan matches. Dad was, and still is, a big fan. Along with another great Cavan supporter, the late, great Connie Lynch of showband industry fame, we travelled Sunday after Sunday around the country to watch the men in blue and white. Were we mad? I am sure many thought so considering the litany of disappointments. There were, and are, more disappointments following Cavan than satisfactory days. They are possibly the Leeds United of the GAA, the glory days well behind them.

There was and is a large Cavan community in Castleknock. It is on the road home to Cavan. Maybe that is why. And the ones that I grew up knowing are all GAA mad. In later years, we filled buses from Castleknock to watch Cavan matches. So I grew up cheering for Cavan. And when I went to Derrylea, I devoured *The Anglo Celt* newspaper every week reading up about Cavan football and club football. My uncle Philip was and is a knowledgeable oracle of Cavan football too, Dad is the youngest of four. Philip is the eldest. Aunties Maureen and Kathleen are in between. Maureen married Aran Island school master Paddy Gill and they lived six or seven miles from Granny's in a place called Ballymachugh on the shores of Lough Sheelin.

During my summers on the farm when I got older, I cycled over to Gills where I had nine cousins, six boys and three girls. Brian, was seven years older than me. And he cycled over to work on the farm. Brian was a big, good-looking man with a great intellect like all his siblings. The Gills were and are well read. Their late dad, Paddy, or Master Gill as he was known, was a bit of an institution highly involved in the GAA, a pioneering founder of the group water scheme and a highly respected local primary school principal.

I looked up to Brian like a big brother and he was great company to have during those hot summer days. Sadly Brian died a young man aged just 37 in 2003 from cancer while living in Australia. He, like all the family, played Gaelic football. The boys played football and the girls camogie and rounders. So there was never a football far away when I went to Gills. We played and played and played with neighbours joining in until it got dark with goal posts made from sticks on a field beside the house that had a slope on it.

Apart from the enjoyment of playing football, be it soccer or gaelic as a 10, 11 and 12 year old, I had a rather unusual obsession whereby I used the back of those large monthly sheets of paper you tore off the butchers calendar hanging on the wall to write down my All-Star team or the best team I had ever seen. Thanks to the influence of my cousins, Peadar,

Padraig and Gerard, I became a Manchester United fan and so kept the scores of their matches too. I was forever playing manager, picking my own best team, keeping a log of scores and statistics from the age of 10 or 11. I would conduct my own mock All Ireland or FA Cup draw. Cavan and Manchester United always did fairly well although both were at the relatively same level of underachieving at the time, the mid-80s.

It was a weird hobby. No doubt. But it helped in the moulding of the career that lay ahead. Peadar claims he remembers my first ever "report". He was over in Granny's and took uncle Philip's old cabless "20" tractor for a spin. And he crashed it. And I went running home shouting: "Granny, Granny, Peadar crashed the tractor!"

Prologue 2
A Leader And A Cub

WHEN my mother's school friend Seamus Darby scored that famous goal for Offaly to snatch a historic fifth consecutive All Ireland from Kerry's grip, the manager of the team was a Longford native called Eugene McGee. He was a sports journalist who had previously managed UCD to success in colleges competition.

He was revered as a messiah in Offaly and had been catapulted to the pinnacle of top managers. Two years later, he was wooed by the Cavan county board chairman at the time, the late Phil Brady. McGee lived a stones throw from Arva where Phil Brady ran a car dealership and was one of the best known businessmen in the county. He convinced McGee to take on the challenge of Cavan after the resignation of Gabriel Kelly, who had led Cavan to an Ulster final in 1983 where they lost to Donegal.

I remember wearing one of those blue and white paper hats to Clones that day. We were beside the press box and Dad urged me to go over to shake Micheal O'Hehir's hand. He was commentating on the game. Ironic then that about 20 years later, I performed the sideline reporter role for RTÉ Radio working with that legend of Irish broadcasting, Mícheál Ó Muircheartaigh, at the Ulster final. That day in 1983, Seamus Bonner was the Donegal hero. Martin McHugh was the up-and-coming star of Gaelic football. In subsequent years I would become friends with both and, in fact, was honoured to deliver the eulogy at Seamus's funeral in 2012.

Back in 1984, Eugene McGee to me was like what Brian Cody is to a young Kilkenny fan or Jim Gavin to a Dub today. I remember his first match in charge, a Division Three league match against Leitrim in Breffni Park in the autumn of '84. I was at an age when my interest in sport was being moulded. By the age of 11 you have a fair idea what your sport of choice is going to be. For me, it was Gaelic football followed by soccer and snooker. Since then my interest in aspects of the green baize has been replaced by a strong interest in hurling, athletics and rugby which I have developed over the years alongside my two favourites Gaelic football and soccer.

McGee managed Cavan for four years with relative success although no elusive provincial title which the once Kings of Ulster had last annexed in 1969. Around this time, McGee opened *The Cavan Leader* newspaper. It was modelled on the well established mother ship, the long-established *Longford Leader*, of which he was owner and editor-in-chief. A young whipper snapper journalist from Lanesboro, County Longford called Ciaran Mullooly was installed as editor.

On a Wednesday night during the summer, I cycled into Ballyjamesduff to get *The Cavan Leader*. It had to steal a march on its much bigger competitor, the long famed *Anglo Celt*, which printed on a Thursday. But with McGee in charge of the county team, the *Leader* had plenty to offer the avid Cavan fan.

By this stage back in Dublin, the Cavan GAA Supporters Club had been established by a group of diehards. Supporters Clubs were all the rage particularly in Dublin where the ex-pat money was. Tipperary were the pioneers. Their modus operandi was to help fundraise for the county board while also acting as a social club for like-minded fanatics.

Dad was involved as was most Dublin based Cavan businesspeople. Builders and publicans made up the bulk of the Cavan businesses in Dublin, fairly rich pickings so for an only too delighted county board. Dad had just bought The Roselawn Inn pub in Castleknock after 20 years managing the famous Harp Bar on O'Connell Bridge. The Roselawn became a hub for the Cavan Supporters Club which was exciting for me. The annual player of the year award was hosted there and all of the Cavan players would be in attendance with me serving them pints. There were quizzes, race-nights and golf classics and I took on the job of sending off the "Cavan Supporters Club (Dublin Branch) news" by post to *The Cavan Leader* once a month or so.

In building the papers GAA coverage which included the all important GAA club notes page, Ciaran Mullooly had made contact with Michael Martin, the secretary of the supporters club, looking for news of our events, a job which was delegated my way. It was my first time to see my name in print. Yes, the two or three paragraph notice board had my byline! Little did I know then I would end up as best man for Ciaran Mullooly and his wife Angela O'Reilly from Mullahoran whom he met while both were working in the *Leader*.

So you could say penning these sporadic newsletter-like notes of the Cavan Supporters Club (Dublin Branch) was the beginning of my career. Like the trickle that must begin somewhere to give us the River Nile, writing those 100 word notes was the real sowing of the seed. The excitement of seeing my name in print was the clincher. I wanted to be a match reporter, a journalist.

My mind was fixated. I got brave and wrote to Eugene, to ask if I could spend a week on work experience in *The Cavan*

Leader. It was the beginning of summer in 1989 and I was 16, an age when most of us are asked to start getting out and earning some pocket money.

I was still spending the summer in Ballyjamesduff helping out on the farm, half-enjoying myself, half-working and didn't really want to give that up. But I posted the letter to McGee anyway. Some days later, the phone rang in Granny's.

"Damien?".

"Yes, speaking."

"Hello, this is Eugene McGee here." I nearly let the phone fall on the floor.

I had seen McGee on TV on shows like the *Sunday Game* many times and so he was sort of famous in my mind. And I didn't know many famous people. Yet here he was talking to me on first name terms. He invited me to spend a week in the *Leader* offices in Cavan.

My heart was pounding with excitement. I was 16 and I was going to Cavan town to work in a newspaper. But Granny was sad. I was great company for her. Granny was born in 1895 and died in her 100th year in 1994. She reared me like a child of her own and spoilt me, giving me money and loved having me around the place.

She was a great storyteller and told me tales which were personal to her but were really history lessons as well. Stories about friends she knew who perished on the Titanic. There was the one of the black and tans raiding her house. And, of course, she would tell yarns about my father as a child. I was only going 12 miles down the road to Cavan town but it was like a rite of passage and she probably knew that from that summer on, I wouldn't be spending so much of my time on the farm anymore. As it transpired, it was actually a way of guaranteeing that I would spend a lot more time there when I got my first full-time job a few years later.

I stayed with Dad's sister, Kathleen and her husband, Michael in the centre of Cavan town. They were well-known and respected business people and it helped me settle in Cavan by softening my introduction to different people around the town.

I brought my scrapbook of statistics which I had kept, ironically enough, since McGee took over as a Cavan manager. That weird hobby of keeping match programmes and match stats came in handy. I hadn't missed a Cavan league or championship match in five years. My 'homework' every Sunday evening was to collate all the statistics from the game. Teams, subs, scorers and so on. Even to this day, I love perusing old team lineouts and rolls of honour. I must have lost my calling as a sports statistician.

So on day one in the *Leader*, in wanting to write a story, I set about tabling all of the stats which included a list of about 60 players who had donned the blue and white jersey in league and championship over the previous half decade. I had all the match results, scorers and I remember even being able to outline the amount of times that Cavan matches had been featured on RTÉ television in those primitive *Sunday Game* times.

I sent them to Eugene McGee in Longford where the paper was mocked up and edited. This was pre-internet days so all the copy went on the three o'clock bus from Cavan to Longford every Tuesday evening. When the paper arrived into the office the following day, there was a big double page spread with "By Damien O'Reilly" and my pen pic beside it. Like a gambler winning big, the buzz was immense. This is what I want to be.

Beside the piece, McGee wrote an editorial and described my article as "excellently researched". A week or two later, I met him in person for the first time. He had this habit of not looking at you when he spoke to you. He was a straight down the line sort of man. He stood with his back to the wall and hands tapping the radiator behind his legs and looking down at his feet, he said: "You have a great aptitude". Then he added something about "being mad in the head" to want to be a journalist. But it's a snapshot in time which I remember and which gave me a great boost.

I ended up staying the summer and on my last Friday, when the envelope with all the pay cheques arrived into the Farnham Street office of *The Cavan Leader* from head office in Longford, I recall the receptionist Ann Donoghue shouting excitedly down the corridor that there was one for me too.

I opened it up. And there it was handwritten. Pay Damien O'Reilly, £100. Signed. Eugene McGee. I photocopied it for posterity. It is probably in a box in the attic of my parents house today.

The following summer I did my Leaving Cert in O'Connells CBS off Dublin's North Circular Road, just behind Croke Park. It would have been easier to get into Trinity College to study medicine then than into the Journalism College in Rathmines. I wasn't bad at school but nowhere near the genius territory required to accumulate enough points to go to Rathmines. Mercifully, a new journalism course had just started in Senior College, Ballyfermot. Following another summer in *The Cavan Leader* where I was allowed to drive the "*Leader* van" to cover club matches, I applied to get into Ballyfermot. They weren't so much interested in my Leaving Cert results. More what interest I had in journalism. "Well, just wait 'til I show you."

I remember smiling as I opened my portfolio of articles from *The Cavan Leader*, My name, My picture. And a gushing reference from Eugene McGee. Brenda Hartnett who was my interviewer and in charge of the Broadcast Journalism Skills course in Ballyfermot was suitably impressed and I was offered a place on the two year diploma course as my mother waited outside in the car park. I skipped out and told her that I would be starting college there in September studying journalism. Now this was for real.

Unlike a university, we were a small group. We played soccer at lunchtime. Sometimes we ventured across to a little pub in Ballyfermot and drank beer until our money ran out and then we would all go our separate ways

Prologue 3
Going 'Live To Air',
Working In The Real World

BILL DUMPLETON was a very interesting man. Not least because of his most unusual name. But he was the senior technician at Dunsink Observatory which was a 15 minute cycle up a twisty hill from my house in Castleknock over towards Finglas.

I was in primary school with Bill's son Liam. And then we were in secondary school together. And then we both got into Ballyfermot senior college together. Every second Saturday night, there was an open night at Dunsink which Bill conducted. I'd cycle up and you could listen to him all night talking about literally the sun, the moon and the stars.

Liam and I became great friends and in late September 1990, we got the bus together for the first time across the relatively new M50 which connected both sides of the Liffey Valley to Ballyfermot.

O'Connell's was an all boys school. Now I was in a mixed classroom. So I stocked up on the deodorant and hair gel! It was a really great place and I made friends for life. Unlike a University, we were a small group. We played soccer at lunchtime. Sometimes we ventured across to a little pub in Ballyfermot and drank beer until our money ran out and then we would all go our separate ways. I was in my element as I was mixing with similar minded contemporaries. Politics, sport and the media were our interests. Among ourselves we never stopped talking. All of us with strong opinions. That is a gaggle of journalists for you. Opinionated so and so's!

We were grilled in the basics of radio and journalism. Local radio was relatively new at the time. Some of my classmates, equivalent to my experience in *The Cavan Leader*, had experience from working in the pirate stations which had sprung up around the country. They were being closed down at that time and replaced with new licenced stations. It was exciting times in the radio sphere with job opportunities on the horizon.

At the end of this two-year course, we got some sort of a diploma as we headed into the real world of adulthood. We had, as part of the course, some radio training. In fact, we were given a licence by the then equivalent of the BAI (Broadcasting Authority of Ireland) to broadcast a college radio station for one week. 'SCB FM.'

Somewhat by accident, I was given the job of presenting one of the programmes, a political debate-type show. There was an almighty row when the late Jim Mitchell had a right barney with a local Sinn Féin activist. Back then, Sinn Féin was politically persona non gratis. They were due to have their Ard Fhéis in some local community centre and there was uproar, allowing these "IRA sympathisers" the use of the hall. And Deputy Mitchell was scathing in his disapproval. Here I was in the middle of a row Vincent Browne would have been proud of.

And I loved it as I practised my best Jeremy Paxman style. Duck to water. I was falling more in love with this radio business than I was with any notion of being a sport's scribe. Justin Treacy and Ryle Nugent of RTÉ Sport fame were in my class. Justin and I became great buddies, so much so, we thumbed a lift to the Rose Of Tralee festival that first summer of college. There were many others in our class who went on to bigger and better things in the world of journalism and broadcasting including Ciaran O'Byrne, who now sits five feet away from me as a producer on Mary Wilson's *Drivetime*. Turns out we weren't a half bad class after all.

During the summer of 1992, having finished my college course, I remember playing golf one sunny evening with Dad in Westmanstown Golf Club when like a wallop it hit me. I distinctly remember the sinking feeling in my stomach as, for some reason, while I was enjoying the round of golf, I was punched with this horrible depressing feeling. It said: "It's time you got a job!" But where?

I had fleetingly thought about continuing with some other degree course as the Ballyfermot course only yielded a relatively lowly ranking third level qualification. But that wasn't going to butter any parsnips and I didn't want to burden my parents with further financial outlays.

Just as the worry was setting in and a sense of panic, I spotted an opportunity. *The Hogan Stand* was the name of a new weekly GAA magazine. I wrote to the editor, sending my CV and I kept my fingers crossed something might come of it. Within days, John Lynch rang me and asked to meet. I couldn't believe it. The timing was perfect. A match made in heaven. Writing about GAA for a living? Happy days!

There was zero journalism in our family. Unlike so many others who would follow in their father's footsteps, I was a bit of a freak. Lots of journalists are sons or daughters of journalists. Farmers are sons and daughters of farmers. Chemists are the sons and daughters of chemists. And so on and so on. My Dad was a publican. My two brothers followed him into the pub trade but I had two left feet when it came to serving pints. I am far better suited the other side of the counter, like so many in the journalism business!

Dad had been the manager and director of the Harp Bar on O'Connell Bridge. Back in the day The Harp was a focal point in Dublin city. It was frequented by many famous people. Dad has stories of famous musicians, politicians and sports people who were customers and who he got to know personally. It was also a watering hole for many well-known scribes from the papers, the *Irish Press*, *The Irish Times* and the *Irish Independent*. There were plenty of pubs of choice for the hacks to quench their thirst in this pocket of the city centre and The Harp happened to be one of them. And no better clientele to keep the till ringing than journalists. Legendary in one sense. Sad in another.

The late Con Houlihan was one of them. Dad and Con were friends despite Con's shyness in public. One night, Dad brought home a copy of the *Evening Press* where Con had penned a column centred around Dad and his love of Cavan football. When Dad was leaving The Harp, there was a big party and many well-known hacks and GAA people were in attendance. That was in 1989 and I was in awe of all these guys whose reports and columns I read. So that was really the only exposure I had to journalism, Dad's friendship with hacks like Con Houlihan and others. He would often get the inside line on a story that was making the news.

We would be at home watching the news and there would be some high profile story making the headlines. Dad would say: "Wait till I tell you the real story there". He would have been given the inside track by a couple of journos just back from the Four Courts or a Garda crime scene. This sort of excitement about the job of being a reporter had an impact on me. Many newspapers and PR companies had launches in The Harp. And Dad was no slouch either at using the papers, Louis Walsh-style, to get publicity. This included the photo of Dad and two attractive female staff from The Harp posing in the *Evening Press* with a set of crutches a customer had left behind. Dad wasn't one to miss a trick. So he was onto one of the photographers a few doors down Burgh Quay! I just bought into all that razzmatazz.

I met John Lynch in a pub in Carnaross in County Meath close to *The Hogan Stand* offices. Well when I say offices, I mean a collection of portakabins behind the Lynch family homestead outside the village of Crossakiel. John was one of a large family who were nearly all working for the magazine and other titles which fell under the umbrella of Lynn Publications.

The meeting was a success. I was just what John needed. My Cavan GAA interest had come to my rescue as the Lynches had close connections with Cavan although being staunchly Meath. But the fact I had a grá for the GAA at local level, that I understood rural Ireland, rubbed off John well. I would start the job the following Monday.

I ran out to find a kiosk to ring home with the good news as I couldn't wait the hour journey to let Mam and Dad know that I was all grown up now. That was September 1992. I was 19 and here I was working full time. My first pay cheque was for £127. After three months it rose to £140 a week. I wore a double-breasted petrol blue suit for my first day in work. On Tuesday and subsequently, I wore a pair of jeans and a T-shirt to the portakabin office behind the house, next door to the Lynch farm down that narrow country road halfway between Crossakiel and Kilskyre. The ex-Meath footballer and local Jody Devine sold ads for *The Hogan Stand*. He gave me Paul Curran's number five jersey which he had swapped with him that year to wear when I stood on Hill 16 to witness Donegal beat Dublin in the 1992 All Ireland final.

That must have been my rebellious years or else it was as a result of working among Meath people, that I turned to supporting my home county Dublin in the final. Not that I would ever shout against Dublin except when they play Cavan, but I had a Hill ticket and so went the full distance by wearing a jersey. I hadn't a Dublin jersey so I borrowed one. That it was Paul Curran's was a bonus. Sheepishly, I gave it back to Jody on the Monday morning after Dublin's defeat to Donegal.

Jody and I used to go into Kells every day for our lunch. Everyone in Kells knew Jody, who was a bit of a local hero. Here I was again in awe of fame. I really was like the journalist equivalent of a band groupie or a hanger on. Journalism and being within touching distance of these sort of famous people was like a fix in hindsight.

Prologue 4
Writing On The Wall

MANY young and aspiring journalists often contact me wondering how they can get into RTÉ or into journalism. The media landscape has changed rapidly in recent years and is under serious pressure. Would I encourage my daughter or son to follow my footsteps? The short answer is 'no.' But for those that have the ambition to work in radio or publishing, you have got to start at the very bottom and work your way up. You must learn the ropes preferably at a local level, like I did. That remains the case. Like devilling to be a barrister, be prepared to work hard and for very little.

When I was in *The Cavan Leader*, even at the age of 16, I was going to County Council meetings and district court sittings. That is the foundation or the bread and butter of journalism. Understanding local government and the judicial system is a must for anyone who wants to write or broadcast even if it is fashion or sport in which you wish to specialise. A wage of £127 a week didn't go too far even back in 1992 but it was a start and you couldn't put a value on such experience. Like a snowball effect, my experience in *The Cavan Leader* led to the college course which in turn led to me getting my foot in the door at *The Hogan Stand* too, my GAA interests notwithstanding. I had a foot on the ladder.

The Hogan Stand premises were situated behind a small bungalow house down a country road surrounded by fields of cattle, about a mile outside Crossakiel which itself was about

10 miles south of Oldcastle on the Cavan-Meath border. Fortunately I didn't have to go searching for digs.

It was a fair spin from Castleknock to Crossakiel. So, naturally enough, I was going back to Ballyjamesduff. Granny was delighted. It took me about 40 minutes from there to Crossakiel. My mother had given me her white two door Volkswagen Golf and I paid in instalments for it. Add in petrol and I wasn't exactly hitting the nightclubs around Dublin at the weekends with what I had left.

I thought that I was naturally made to write for *The Hogan Stand*. Truth was, I wasn't. And I had many chats with John about some of the articles I was writing. I think I was trying too hard to be eccentric. What I thought was pure art was what others might have thought pure muck. I wasn't keeping it simple enough and John was losing his mind trying to tell me to just keep it simple. It wasn't rocket science to write a story about a former inter-county goalkeeper and his thoughts on his county's chances in the upcoming championship But that is exactly what I was trying to do, turn it into rocket science.

To keep me employed, John had an idea. He got me to sell ads. He thought I had a voice to sell ads. And I hated it. I was embarrassed squeezing money out of small business people like my dad who had bigger things to worry about than putting in an ad to wish the local team well. This was pre-boom years after all and money was scarce.

One week I was given a list of businesses in Cavan to call with an invitation to place an ad in some Cavan focussed feature. I knew many of the people I was phoning. I had no choice but to ring them as I had a target to reach. I changed my accent and called myself some other name to try and disguise myself. Drastic times require drastic measures.

"Would you like to place an ad?".

"No thanks".

"Alright, bye bye".

I had no will to try and arm twist and I was going in every day to sift through a list of businesses to call. A bit like how I felt on the golf course almost a year earlier, I was getting anxious and felt I was spiralling into a dark hole. I couldn't envisage doing this for the rest of my life. And my writing was not what I thought it was. It led yet again to the question – "What am I going to do?"

*It was like being a
kid in a sweet shop.
I just felt this warm sense
of excitement being
inside the radio
station building*

Prologue 5
Something In The Air

NORTHERN Sound Radio was the local station in Cavan. When I was in *The Cavan Leader*, a man called Phelim Cox sold ads but he was also a part time DJ with Northern Sound and a living legend on the radio. He was the happiest man you could meet and was wonderful company. Larger than life and an all round gentleman. His grandson, Evan Walsh, is now part of the up and coming Cavan band, The Strypes.

During those two summers in the *Cavan Leader*, I travelled with him in his little Fiat Panda from Cavan to Monaghan where the Northern Sound studios were situated to mooch around, getting to know the faces behind the voices I was listening to on the wireless. I am indebted to Phelim, who passed away a few years ago, for allowing me do this as it gave me a timely taste of the radio business which I would otherwise not have been able to experience easily. It is why I am always only too happy to show an aspiring broadcaster around RTÉ whenever they ask.

It was like being a kid in a sweet shop. I just felt this warm sense of excitement being inside the radio station building. I got to know the sports guys including the stations commentator Michael Tynan from Virginia in Cavan. I had actually known Michael before then but now I was interested in doing what he was doing. He asked me if I would like to do some match reports. Would I what? So during the summer of 1990, I did report from a couple of club matches. They were terrible reports but it was all a learning curve.

Northern Sound was not too well got in Cavan. Listeners

felt that it was "all about Monaghan". When I say listeners, I was talking about my relations and friends around Cavan who would often sigh: "Ah it's all Monaghan, Monaghan, Monaghan". It is a problem all local radio stations spanning more than one county face and must deal with. But there was some truth in what people were saying in Cavan. That was because the newsroom was based in Monaghan town, a wee shop across the street from the Garda Station, and most of the people broadcasting were from Monaghan.

Apart from Phelim and Michael Tynan, there was no other Cavan influence I can distinctly remember. And nobody was covering local authority meetings in Cavan. That is a bit like a newspaper not having reporters at half the weekend matches. The word was that the bosses knew it and they needed to find someone who would be able to cover local authority meetings and other routine events around Cavan. I can't recollect for sure, but I must have let it be known to someone who knew someone that I was in the market for a bit of radio work and I was the answer to their problems.

And so one evening out of the blue, the phone rang in Granny's. It was Pauline McKenna, head of news at Northern Sound. She had gotten my contact number in Ballyjamesduff somewhere which is what we had to do then to contact people as there was no other way back then. They were looking for someone to report on Cavan stories. I got the impression that it was a sort of part-time stringer they were looking for. It wasn't ideal. I would need better than that but I agreed to go and meet her and her bosses.

Northern Sound had merged with the much more successful Shannonside Radio which covered Roscommon, Longford and south Leitrim. The group headquarters was along the Sligo road outside Longford. I was invited by Pauline to meet the Chief Executive, John Morrin and station manager Joe Finnegan. I set off to meet them in the same petrol-blue double-breasted suit I'd met John Lynch in about 12 months earlier. *The Hogan Stand* office was a portakabin. The Shannonside Northern Sound HQ was an old country estate called Minard House, a mile outside Longford town.

It was actually a sort of job interview. I was even left alone for 20 minutes to do an unexpected exam. I was given a newspaper story and told to rewrite it for radio. I hadn't a clue what I was doing but it worked. Now I was actually being offered more than just a part-time reporter's job. I was being offered a full-time job presenting the sports news, the weekend sports shows, a weekday current affairs show, reading the farm news and reporting on council meetings in Cavan. Yesssss! As it turned out, I was never off the radio between all of those commitments.

A year after getting a great start from John Lynch and the Lynch family, I told him I was leaving. He wasn't surprised and reckoned I was going to my natural calling. And he couldn't have been more supportive. He was a sound mentor. We had a bit of a going away party in Jody Devine's parents pub down the road in Kilskyre.

I started working in Northern Sound in October 1993. They refurbished their studio in Cavan town and at last Cavan would have a voice of their own on radio. It was hellish work but I loved it. Initially, I was on my own in the Cavan studio. Soon, I was joined by a receptionist and a sales rep. And naturally my residence didn't change. Now I only had a 12 mile journey from Ballyjamesduff to Cavan town while at weekends, I broadcast the sports programmes from the mother ship in

Longford. I made great friends for life. People like Seamus Duke, Fintan Duffy and James Healy all broadcasters of note. Grainne Gormley was another who I remain friendly with to the present day.

Declan McBennett, who is one of the heads in RTÉ News and Justin Treacy of RTÉ Sport, also worked there in my time. When I left in 1998, a young eager guy called Fran McNulty took over the farm news duties. Fran is now a well-known voice and face on RTÉ News. Before I arrived in '93, Ciaran Mullooly had been and gone, to RTÉ. I was following him around it seems. After I left, several other national reporters and journalists served their time in Shannonside/Northern Sound!

And then there was Owen McConnon. Owen was a commentator working with BBC Radio Ulster. He was from Cavan and I knew Owen for many years through my Dad and Connie Lynch. Connie was a co-founder of the Jimmy Magee All Stars. Their first ever match was in Ballyjamesduff on June 6, 1966. The sixth of the sixth nineteen sixty six. Dad still regales us with stories about driving the likes of Brendan Bowyer and other showband heroes from Dublin to that occasion. Owen, a talented musician in his own right and friend of Connie, got involved in the All Stars in subsequent years.

He had also done the odd gig for Northern Sound as a talented broadcaster himself and he became a great mentor to me in those first broadcasting months. We travelled to many Cavan training nights in Ballyhaise together to interview the players. When Martin McHugh became manager, the profile of the county lifted. Owen and I were always given priority by McHugh when it came to getting interviews. To this day, Owen, Martin and I often meet for a pint and reminisce.

Again the pay at Northern Sound was fairly pitiful but I survived. This was the radio career I wanted. Over the next four years and seven months, I cut my teeth in radio. There were a few failed interviews and applications for jobs in RTÉ but I stuck at it and eventually in May 1998, I finally made it. Six years earlier in a mock interview in Ballyfermot, I was asked by Liam Dumpleton during one of our TV modules, where would I like to see myself in 10 years' time. "RTÉ", was my immediate reply. I achieved that goal with four years to spare and was now packing my bags in Ballyjamesduff to go home to Castleknock.

The job in RTÉ was in the now-defunct "Agricultural department". I had done a successful interview to be put on a panel and as jobs came up for grabs I would get a call. That call came sooner rather than later. I was the only one on the panel who had experience working in "agriculture". Ironically I had played down my farm news experience in favour of pushing my experience in sport, politics and current affairs, areas I would have far preferred to delve into ahead of agriculture. Yet it was the farm news part of my CV which was now pushing open the big door into RTÉ.

I felt I had bluffed my way through many of the farm news bulletins which I read thrice daily on Shannonside/Northern Sound often reverting to my uncle Philip for clarity on various complex farming stories. The day I mentioned the "sentimental" cattle sale was not one of my better days reading farm news. Of course, the sale was of Simmental cattle. Now in the big beast of the national broadcaster, I would have to pull up my socks.

I thought that once I got a foot in the door, I'd eventually nudge Des Cahill out of the way and move into the sports department. Well, it didn't happen and 19 years later during which the way farm news is broadcast had gone through many metamorphoses, I am still I suppose working mainly in the "agricultural department". And regrets? I have none.

Countrywide was born in September 2009. I had been presenting a programme called *Farmweek*, a half-hour recorded programme every Saturday morning. First I begged RTÉ to move it from the sleepy time of 7.30am to 8.30am. And then I begged the station to allow me to go live. The answer was 'yes' but on condition that I change the name of the programme to reflect the interests of a broader audience. I was reluctant as I felt that the great traditions of farm news broadcasting in RTÉ had been dumbed down enough over the years. This was a further move away from that tradition. Eventually I saw their point which was that a name like *Farmweek* would alienate a large portion of the available audience. It would also reduce the range of topics and stories we could cover.

And that is how *Countrywide* came about and has become one of the most listened to programmes on national radio during the past eight years. It also gave me a greater profile in media circles particularly among the farming audience. A year later in 2010, as a result of being a reporter strongly connected with farming and rural matters, another door opened when the editor of *Irish Country Living* in the *Farmers Journal*, Mairead Lavery, called me. Darragh McCullough was leaving his post in the *Farmers Journal*. He wrote a weekly column called Darragh's Diary. It would now become Damien's Diary.

Writing a weekly column can be a challenge. Some weeks the columns almost write themselves. Other week's not so. But during the past seven years, there have been over 350 Damien's

Diaries published. It's an opinion piece and opinion divides. We all have opinions. We all have our views. Some weeks, people pull me up on what I have to say. Other weeks, they congratulate me.

But I never set out to insult, infuriate or isolate. As a writer, you cannot predict how any one person or group might interpret what you are trying to say. And sometimes, a throwaway line can infuriate and create an online onslaught which can totally be disproportionate to the actual tone of the piece. It is a dilemma for journalists to weigh up, having the nerve not to fear what some people might think of what you have to say or write, even if you are trying to stick to the basics which is to be fair and accurate. It is a big debate in the current era of "fake news" wars which has taken on a whole new life courtesy of President Donald Trump

Critical analysis, investigative journalism, personal opinion, satire and observation make up some of the key ingredients of journalism. Yet in the modern world of social media and so called citizen journalism which in part, is on the warpath with the so called mainstream media, if you cut close to the bone on an issue or story with a comment, opinion or observation, you run the risk of a tsunami of unchecked unbridled and sometimes organised campaigning online fury. To receive an angry letter or email questioning your credentials on foot of something you said or something you wrote has to be taken on the chin, even if it rocks self-esteem.

You cannot expect to be a broadcaster or journalist asking questions, reporting news or giving opinion on a public forum without now and again expecting a polar questioning view from your listeners or your readers who are essentially your loyal customers. And when a reader or a listener writes a letter in disagreement with something you have written or broadcast, and signs their name to it, you have to take that hit. If it is not signed, well, you take it, but with a sprinkling of scepticism. I have received many the angry, swear-laden letters about something I had said or written and on the odd occasion, something I hadn't said or written. And I like them. Because anyone nowadays that sits down with a pen and paper to have a go at you, buys a stamp and goes to the trouble of posting it has to be admired! And if they put their name and address to it, I try if required, to respond.

However, when it comes in the form of vulgar, defaming and personal abuse online, often from nameless people, it can be unnerving, even if you accept that it is just part and parcel of the modern world. People in the public eye are always in the firing line. That includes journalists who admittedly do enjoy the privilege of a public platform to air personal opinion. But even when you are reasonable and accurate in your comments and reporting, such is the way of the world now, you are fair game for the keyboard warriors and blinkered campaigners with a prejudice. I was told recently as I was conducting a live interview, two texts came in from listeners within seconds. One accused me of being right wing, the other accused me of being left wing. I took that as a win, win for me!

Taking the rough with the smooth is the nature of the job. There are times when I come out of the studio after a show or when I sit down and read back a column, that I feel I am in the wrong job.

Yet I wouldn't be at anything else. If I left RTÉ tomorrow, I would miss the buzz terribly. But I would probably get over it. However, I don't think I could ever put down the pen. Even on holidays, my laptop is with me. Now I know why children get so much fun from a colouring book and crayons. What I do now is the grown up version of what I was doing, scribbling fantasy All Ireland draws and All Star teams on the back of the butcher's calendar. And so it has been a great privilege and opportunity to pen Damien's Diary for the *Farmers Journal* and the urge to bundle the best of them in a book has gotten the better of me. But the journey has been fascinating.

There were two shops my grandmother visited every Friday to do her shopping, Murphys and Langtrys. There were two brown boxes. The old way of doing your shopping was to hand in your list and the box would be filled with your groceries. All the while, you stood at the counter and the shopkeeper would gather the items one by one. The tea, bread, butter and sugar and the like were sourced in Murphys. The more bespoke items such as the sweets I loved were to be got in Langtrys. The local butchers of course for all the meat and fish. Friday was shop day. And that included Philip picking up the *Anglo Celt* and the *Farmers Journal*.

There wasn't much for me to read about in the Journal but that changed bit by bit as I got older. It was a bible. My uncle Philip never went a week without it. He was one of tens of thousands. It seems to me that you could have gone without certain things but not the *Farmers Journal*. I think that is still the way in a lot of farmsteads across the land.

I'm honoured to be part of that publication and my columns include observations of contemporary stories and issues which face us all. I try to call things as I see them and the opinions are not the Journals or RTÉ's but my own.

I have given this insight into my background as an introduction to the columns I have penned on the back page of *Irish Country Living*. I hope it also explains how I have ended up here, a city boy with a country view.

*There is a GAA club
in Roscommon called
St Faithleach's. And I had
just read out a match result
involving them completely
oblivious to the distinction
between the spelling and
the pronunciation*

Radio Days

My Exclusive 'Sentimental Sale' Gaff

I started work in Shannonside/Northern Sound in the autumn of 1993. But it wasn't all plain sailing. Whatever about being awkward behind the bar, there have been many awkward moments behind the microphone too.

The phones were hopping and the rage was palpable. "Will you tell that clown that it's not pronounced 'Faithlocks'; it's pronounced 'Fallyahs.'

I was only a week in my new job. It was a Sunday evening and I was reading out the local GAA results on Shannonside Radio. There is a GAA club in Roscommon called St Faithleach's. And I had just read out a match result involving them completely oblivious to the distinction between the spelling and the pronunciation. It was an early and blunt reminder of the main pitfall of working in radio, which is that you must never, ever make a mistake of any description.

Because if you do, you will be lit upon. Like the way I was in more recent times when a listener went bananas because I had apparently – as the listener had heard it – pronounced Volkswagen as "Vollswagen". Yes, listeners can be even that pedantic too!

But in the case of the GAA club in Roscommon, listeners were right to be annoyed. It taught me a salutary lesson that the correct pronunciations of town-lands, villages and towns is paramount to pretty much everything when it comes to working on radio.

There is really no excuse for mispronouncing Clones, Balla, Granard and Castlerea, yet it still happens and it annoys people. Then, of course, there are the funny on-air mistakes and believe me I've had a few howlers in my time.

Once when reading out the death notices in my local radio days, I came across a notice which I had already read out. In other words, it was mistakenly entered twice on the list. As I was about to read it out again, I stumbled and uttered sombrely: "I'm afraid he is dead already." Another colleague on discovering that there were actually no deaths to read out one evening proceeded to play the jingle for the company sponsoring the death notices. In a last minute panic, he felt he ought to play the jingle seeing that the company were paying good money for it and nobody had ever envisaged a day when there would not be at least one person in the region to pass on. Once the jingle finished, he apologised to listeners that there were no deaths to bring but that he "hoped" to have some death notices for the next bulletin!

On another occasion, reading the farm news, I read out the word bullocks but with an O sound instead of a U, if you get my drift.

Staying with matters bovine on local radio, I left a colleague in charge of reading farm news one evening. He admitted that he would barely know the difference between a bull and a heifer but I assured him that all he had to do was read what was written in front of him. He duly obliged by informing listeners of the availability of the local AI service over a particular bank holiday weekend, except he read it out as "the A-one man".

Not to be outdone, I had the job one evening of telling listeners about a special dispersal sale due to take place the following day in Edgeworthstown. A local farmer had paid dearly for this ad to go out on radio in order to attract as many buyers as possible to the sale. Again, young and wet behind the ears, I informed listeners that there would be "a special dispersal sale of sentimental heifers at Edgeworthstown mart at two o'clock tomorrow."

The following afternoon, one listener called in to inform us that indeed, yes, several heifers were seen crying and hugging each other outside the mart following a very 'sentimental' sale!

*   *   *

Power Of A Simple 'Sorry For Your Troubles'

There was a time when the weather forecast or the news were the most important dates which country people in particular kept with their radio on a daily basis. But over the past 20 years or so the death notices have become the main draw for radio listeners, mainly in rural Ireland.

It's a reflection of the unique Irish tradition of funeral-going and paying respects that the death notices attract the peak audience. In the first chapter of his book, 'Life, Death and Hurling,' former Offaly hurler Michael Duignan writes very movingly about the passing of his wife Edel in September 2009. His account of how the local community rallied around is something most people who have suffered bereavement – particularly in rural Ireland – will immediately identify with.

The wake, the sandwiches, the car parking attendants, the guard of honour, the post-funeral gathering, I don't want to sound flippant about it but the Irish funeral is a part of Irish culture which can be reassuring at a time of terrible bereavement and the snapshot provided by Duignan of the process in action at a terrible time for his family is spot on.

When my own grandmother died tragically in a car accident while on holiday in the USA in 2004, my uncle Mike Pagella, an American married to my mother's sister Marie in Florida, was gobsmacked by the whole process, from the wake to the removal to the funeral.

It was something you just would not see where he comes from. Sure, people will sympathise and commiserate but in a much more formal way. I still smile when I remember people coming up to him in the church and commiserating. He didn't really know how to react but found the whole process most comforting at a very tough time for his wife and all of the family.

Here, people sit into their cars and drive for hours just to shake hands and pay respects. And I have never come away from a church, funeral home or burial house after spending no more than five minutes there, thinking that I had wasted time. It means so much to people to see friends and colleagues make the effort to take time out and show their respects.

Back in 2004, I remember standing by my grandmother's coffin and seeing the queue of people coming into the house. Many of them had travelled great distances to spend 10 seconds in our company and say: "Sorry for your troubles."

More recently a good friend and neighbour of our family, Johnjoe Reilly, died in Ballyjamesduff. Within an hour of his remains being brought back to be waked, I called to the house. Already there were neighbours in hi-vis jackets directing traffic while others were calling with food and drink. The house was full at 10 o'clock with neighbours and friends there to help out and give Johnjoe the sort of farewell he deserved after 88 years of life.

It's a tradition which may not be as prevalent in Dublin. I remember once going to the funeral home where the parent of a friend was reposing. My friend, from Dublin, thought this most unusual that I would call to the funeral home. In country areas, it's different. People feel an obligation to rally around. Even though it's a time of immense grief, I know very few people who dislike the process of having people call, particularly when the alternative is to have very few around you at such a trying time.

Now, will you ever turn up the radio there – the deaths are coming on.

*   *   *

Eulogies – To Ban Or Not To Ban

When I die, I don't want a eulogy. Cut the bull and get it over with in as straightforward a way as possible. No bells and whistles. But then that's me.

When I hit the big four-o in 2013 it was just like any other day. These milestone events tend to send some people into a tizzy of organising surprises and parties, fretting about original and over-the-top presents. I made sure to arrange an interview with a farmer in the far reaches of West Cork that day so as to avoid any of that old bluster about parties and waste-of-money presents. I just don't like the drama of it all.

However, I suppose when it comes to the eulogy, it's out of my hands. I'll be gone a lot further than West Cork, which proves the point that eulogies at funerals are all about those left behind – not the departed.

There was controversy in Meath sometime back over the Bishop's proposal to ban eulogies. Perhaps this move was prompted by churches being hijacked by not too religious people looking for the big send-off for Uncle Mick.

Like any public place, there must be rules and, as cold as it might seem, a bishop surely retains the right to draw up guidelines even when dealing with the delicate subject of bereavement. But in trying to regain control of the church funeral, I think bishops should stop short of a complete ban on eulogies.

I was asked to write and then read a eulogy by the family of a dear friend who died a few years ago. It is not for me to judge, but I hope I did the man and his family justice. I hope I was short and to the point. I hope I didn't come across as a smart-ass and I hope I didn't bore anyone.

Whatever about that occasion, a eulogy, when delivered with clarity and brevity, is no harm. I was at a funeral of a very well-respected man some years ago. His daughter stood up and, flanked by her sisters she read a prepared speech/eulogy of no more than three minutes in which she gave a perfect overview of her dad, where he was from, his loves and his achievements and finished by offering her sincere appreciation to everyone who had helped their family through their tough few days. No long-winded stories. No fondness hearing her own voice. It was adequate and perfect.

It would be a shame if a speech like this was not allowed in future. At some very sad and tragic funerals, dignified eulogies have been delivered by very emotional family members who also shouldn't be denied this option.

But the other extreme is where a family member stands up and starts ranting out of control, trying to be funny, sharing with everyone sometimes embarrassing, irrelevant, boring and even tasteless titbits about the life of the recently departed.

Twenty minute eulogies about someone a lot of people never met, but are there on account of knowing a relative, are not uncommon and frankly they can be terribly embarrassing and inappropriate.

*   *   *

Hurrah For The Smoking Ban

What sadly has sent many loved ones to an early grave is smoking. When I began working in local radio in the nineties, smoking was still the rule rather than the exception. My memory is perhaps as hazy as the newsroom was then, but I would conservatively guess that out of the eight or nine colleagues I can remember working with at the start, all bar one smoked. Me. It didn't take long before I joined the club, but it didn't suit me.

My head would go light at the mere puff of a cigarette but the lure of the nicotine, particularly when out in the pub, was overwhelming. My head would feel like it was about to explode the morning after while the smell of stale ash on my clothes and on my skin, made me retch. I wouldn't think of having a cigarette again until the next night out, unlike the professionals who would reach for one first thing in the morning. I was a pure amateur.

The smoking ban came in but my foolish Mickey Mouse sort of smoking continued where I bummed cigarettes off the professionals. Never during the day. It always took a pint or two to give me the want. Standing outside the pub feeling embarrassed. Feeling awkward and afraid who might see me. No, I wasn't a natural.

But still I continued until one morning a few years back I woke up after a particularly late night, coughing and spluttering with an unusually banging headache. It was the message I needed to summon the willpower to declare never again to inhale a cigarette. And it has worked, proving that it is all in the head. You could blow cigarette smoke in my face now and it wouldn't bother me in the slightest. And I don't pontificate, if you want to smoke, fire ahead.

Thankfully I am not alone in kicking the habit. Over recent years, I have noticed fewer and fewer people smoking. I was at a conference recently, where, among 40 people, two popped out for a smoke at the coffee break. It is anecdotal rather than scientific obviously, but the change in the number of people smoking seems to have been very rapid.

Dr James Reilly may not be fondly remembered for his time as a government minister but he deserves huge credit for the personal crusade he fronted to make Ireland smoke-free by 2025. Advertising and branding has all but been prohibited and from next year packs will carry no branding at all. He did this against the might of the cigarette lobby and stared them down. If I walked into a newsroom now, I am sure that instead of 90 percent being smokers, it would be the other way around. That is some change in two decades and we are all the better for it and both James Reilly and Mícheál Martin have played a huge part in that.

* * *

Dying Art Of Letter Writing

For young journalists entering the business now, it must be difficult for them to understand how the business worked before the internet age. No Google for research purposes and no email. We can communicate in nanoseconds today with people anywhere in the world. But it is not that long ago, we wrote letters.

"Dear Clare". And so began the letter. It was back in the mid-1990s and one of my best friends from college was on a J1 in Boston. During that summer, we kept in touch by post. I'd write to her. A week later the blue and red rimmed Airmail letter would pop through the letterbox from the opposite direction.

There was always great excitement opening the envelope with a long hand-written letter inside. It was nothing more than good friends and I kept those letters for years. But like everything else, God knows where they are now. I would love to read over them again.

And I would also love to read over the letter I sent my mother on the evening of August 10, 1980. Earlier that sweltering summer day, she gave birth to my younger sister Siobhan. True to form, I was on the farm in Cavan and it took a few hours before I received the news. My aunt Maureen came running into the kitchen, hugged me and told me I had a new sister.

There was no phone in Granny's, so I set about writing a letter. I suggested she call my new sister Paula, for some reason. She was named Siobhan Paula. When I was back in Dublin, I would write once a week to my Granny and cycle to the post office in Castleknock to post my letter. The postmistress was from Cavan and always had a good welcome for me. Heck, we even learned in school how to compose a letter, where to put the date and address. Remember that?

But it's a dying art. Last Christmas, I didn't send too many cards. Didn't receive too many either. I suspect though, that while I might be off a few people's Christmas card lists, it is more to do with the fact that Christmas cards, like letters, are an endangered species in the modern age of emails and texts. Why bother writing a letter, licking a stamp and walking to the post-box when you can do all of that on your phone or laptop.

I even mind the old retort to people going abroad: "Don't forget to write." What would a millennial make of that request as they waved loved ones goodbye on their travels? A postcard, what is that? Which reminds me. Sitting in front of the TV one weekend, my old college mate Justin Treacy appeared to read the sports news.

"Daddy, weren't you in college with him?"

"Yes Deirbhile, I was. We were good friends. I remember one summer we thumbed a lift to the Rose of Tralee."

"You. Did. What. Dad?"

Is it really that long since thumbing a lift was commonplace. Clare was also in the same class as Justin and me all those years ago, when we used to write letters and thumb lifts.

* * *

Thumbing – And That Artful Dodger!

As a matter of interest, when was the last time you saw someone thumbing for a lift? I bet it's been a while. I haven't seen anybody do it in years. Alas, another harmless old tradition has disappeared from the roadside.

"How will you get home?"

"Ah, I'll thumb a lift."

A common refrain from yesteryear.

Towns on the edge of Dublin would be lined of a Friday evening with people with a hand outstretched and thumb pointing towards the sky. At Newlands Cross, thumbers took to writing their destination on cardboard, hoping for a kind soul to bring them to far-flung country places.

The thumbers in Blanchardstown on the other hand, if you forgive the pun, were mostly going only to Cavan. You might come across the odd one heading further on to Donegal but in general they didn't require billboards stating the name of their birthplace.

In most cases, thumbers were young people heading home for the weekend. The odd occasion I thumbed, I was the shy, reluctant type who kept the thumb pinned close to the side of my leg in a kind of 'I'm not really thumbing but I wouldn't mind a lift' way.

This contrasted with the extravagant career thumber who would lean out sideways from the footpath, arm fully stretched, thumb sticking away out. There was the fella who walked and thumbed, giving the impression he hadn't far to go. The stating the bleedin' obvious types would wave their thumb in the direction that the driver was going as if he was saying: "Yes, I want to go this way."

And then there was the thumber with the thumb angled downwards or backwards – I never worked out what the message was there.

My father was a great man for giving people lifts as we headed to Cavan through Blanchardstown. If they were destined for anywhere in Cavan and in particular my father's hometown of Ballyjamesduff, it didn't take long for him to work out their seed, breed and generation. Soon after I began driving, I thought I was being the big fella when I stopped one wicked wet wintery evening to offer a desperate-looking thumber a lift. This drenched man was dressed all in black and was thumbing along the side of a dark, twisty road somewhere between Crookedwood and Castlepollard. He was very unkempt and fidgety. He was full of talk, asking loads of questions about where I was from and so on. When I told him where I lived, he asked if I knew many guards around Dublin. As it happened, I did know a good few and began naming them. He nodded knowingly to most of them, especially the ones working in the serious crime unit in Harcourt Street.

"Are you in the force yourself?" I asked.

"Jaysus, no I'm not," he replied.

'So how do you know so many guards then?" I enquired.

"Because I'm a robber," he retorted matter of factly.

At the next crossroads I stopped and told him I was turning off the main road at that point. Eventually after staring at me for what seemed like an eternity, he got out and ran into the darkness. Suffice to say, it put me of stopping for thumbers ever again.

* * *

My Family Kidnap Ordeal With 'The General'

March 10, 1986 – that's the night our family was awoken by armed and masked raiders who broke into our house while we slept.

I woke up at around two o'clock in the morning to hear my mother screaming. I hadn't a clue what was going on so I jumped out of bed and ran into my parents bedroom. Before I could ask or see what was happening, a man dressed in black with a balaclava bundled me back into my own room, which I shared with my two younger brothers, Kenneth and Pauric. They awoke to see this man sitting on our toy snooker table.

I had to pretend that he was a workman painting the house or something along those lines and assured them that everything was alright. The two boys stayed calm as the remaining four men interrogated my parents. When they broke into my parents room, my dad jumped up. Natural reaction, I suppose. They proceeded to hammer the living daylights out of him, breaking his nose, his toes and splitting his head open, knocking him unconscious.

Dad was the manager of the famous Harp Bar on O'Connell Bridge in Dublin city centre at the time. I am sure many country people who came to work in Dublin the 1970s and 80s would have been familiar with the Harp – one of the city's busiest pubs.

The men were looking for the keys of the safe in The Harp. It was probably their intention to take my dad in what we now call a "tiger kidnapping," but they had injured him so badly that they had to revert to Plan B, which was to try to do the job themselves. Hence they remained in our house for several hours, until daybreak.

All the time, they roughed up my parents, shouting at them, demanding time and again information about the safe, where exactly it was, how many keys were needed to get in, what the alarm code was and what the safe code was etc.

After what seemed like ages, they marched my parents into the spare room and tied them up around the bed. We were then marched in one by one and tied up with them. My younger sister, Siobhan, who was five at the time, and her best friend, Niamh O'Mahony, were also awakened and brought in and tied up.

Three of the gang went in to the Harp while the other two thugs stayed with us, warning us in no uncertain terms what would happen if we tried anything. They were all carrying guns. After some time, the house phone rang. This was pre-mobile phone days. It was obviously the others to say that they had done the job. We were warned again not to move. But once we were sure that the other two men had made good their escape, we freed ourselves from the myriad of neckties belonging to Dad which were used to tie us and gag us.

The gang was never caught but it emerged sometime later that the notorious 'General', Martin Cahill was among the five men in our house that night. It was his gang and it was a rare occasion in which he got his own hands dirty. It's just over 30 years since we as a family went through that ordeal, but it's one that I still remember as if it happened yesterday.

The Olympics And My Love Of Sport

Good Enough For Me And Jimmy Magee

We had just landed in Beijing on August 1, 2008 and a half hour later here I was sitting on the shuttle bus with Jimmy Magee, Des Cahill and George Hamilton and the rest of the RTÉ Olympic team as we made our way to our hotel. This must be what it is like for those young soccer players who grew up supporting a team and then finds himself being called up to the first team last minute and on the team bus to a big game. Of course, I knew Jimmy, Des and George and most of the rest of the RTÉ commentary team on the bus. But instead of polishing their football boots, I was now pulling on the team jersey with them.

While not actually competing at the Olympic games, this was the next best thing – working as a reporter at the biggest sporting event on the planet with Jimmy Magee, whose commentary of John Treacy's 1984 silver medal at the LA games was one of my all-time favourite sporting moments, and commentaries. I remember being allowed to stay up late at night during a family holiday in the Isle of Man to watch it on the BBC. We did so on a small television in the resident's room downstairs in the Sunnydale Hotel in Douglas because there were no TVs in the rooms. Jimmy's commentary on RTÉ was so iconic, it was replayed over and over again, as he listed all Ireland's previous Olympic medal wins finishing with that of Treacy's literally as his foot crossed the line. So I only heard it when we got home from the holiday.

But back to Beijing, 24 years later. I had got a late call-up. I was actually in the USA recording a programme in late May 2008 when Roy Willoughby, head of RTÉ Radio sport, rang me to say that they wanted me to go to China.

"When do you need to know, Roy?"

"In about two minutes, Damien," came Roy's reply.

I was on the plane and away from home for four weeks. And tough as it was leaving a young family behind, what a most enjoyable four weeks it was. We were set up in the IBC (International Broadcasting Centre), which was about the same size as Dundrum Shopping Centre in Dublin.

Each day we would go through airport-style security in the lobby of our hotel before boarding our designated shuttle bus to and from the IBC, which was situated beside the Olympic stadium. On the other side of us was a massive windowless building which we were told was being used by the Chinese authorities to listen to our every utterance. (By the way, if you googled Tiananmen Square, you got zero results.)

There were several sporting highlights. I saw Michael Phelps lose. Although he won gold in every event he entered, I saw him come second but still qualify in a semi-final. I was at the Olympic stadium to witness Usain Bolt's amazing 200 metres final. I also sat with Kenny Egan's family during one of his fights.

At one stage I got lost in the middle of Beijing for over two hours and ended up using the sun as navigation back towards base. I bought a set of speakers for my laptop and went through nine personnel in doing so. It was as if I was buying a ground-to-air missile.

I got stuck on the Great Wall during an almighty thunder storm with Des Cahill and Gearoid MacDonncha. And I sat in

Country cousins:
With the Gills — Gerard, Diarmuid, Padraig, Marie and Olivia — around 1977

The country city boy: On the tractor in Ballyjamesduff with uncle Philip (left); and with a rather scary companion back in Dublin

Family ties: At my sister's wedding with (back row) my brothers Kenneth and Pauric and (front row) my parents Pauline and Paddy with Siobhan and her husband Matthew McCormack

Big days out: With Patrick and Deirbhile on Howth Head in summer 2017 (above); and Patrick and Deirbhile standing on the lane outside the farm in Ballyjamesduff where I spent all my holidays at their age

Budding reporter: Patrick doing a little report for me as we broadcast live from Bloom in May 2016

All the Presidents' man: While reporting on a Bord Bia Trade mission to Vietnam in 2016, I bumped into and interviewed former President Mary Robinson (above) who was hosting another event in the same hotel; meeting former President Mary McAleese in Áras an Uachtaráin for an interview about rural isolation (below); and one of the many interviews I have conducted with President Michael D. Higgins (opposite page)

Mayo man: With former Taoiseach Enda Kenny who gave me an interview on the 50th anniversary of the founding of the IFANFA

Old pals: My stand-in on *Countrywide* and RTÉ star Marty Morrissey and I at the Teagasc 1916 commemorative event in Athenry in 2016

Editorial meeting: With Mairead Lavery, editor of the *Irish Country Living* magazine where 'Damien's Diary' appears each week

All smiles: With MEP Mairead McGuinness and Glanbia chairman Henry Corbally at the 2015 Virginia Show

Sideline cuts: Presenting *Sunday Sport* along with pundit and good friend Martin McHugh

Bird's-eye view: Recording the annual pre-Christmas *Countrywide* special at Eastferry poultry farm near Midleton in County Cork in December 2015

a taxi with Jimmy Magee who quizzed the bemused local driver about who he thought would win the Longford senior championship. The driver hadn't a clue what was going on but responded in Chinese anyway with Jimmy interpreting the answers as if the driver was tipping Mostrim to go all the way.

* * *

Barber Of Beijing

When the Beijing games finished, for the first time in a month I had some down time from my duties reporting for RTÉ. We had heard about this amazing barber close to our hotel where you got a two-hour haircut that included an induced snooze – all for about €3. Every day, journalists we got to know from other countries who were staying in our hotel, were returning with heads shaved as if they had been conscripted. And all had the advice to go down the road to the local barber shop.

We had to investigate. Along with a colleague, not exactly endowed with spare tresses that needed trimming, we arrived to be greeted by a platoon of smiling staff, by this stage demonstrably used to this procession of foreign sports reporters looking for a haircut, whether they needed one or not. Talk about doing the business by word of mouth.

After a royal welcome, eventually I was brought to an elaborate sink where my hair was washed, washed and washed again. Either it was badly in need of such washing or else this was a novelty, washing fair hair, but my host wasn't going to present me to the next stage without a glistening mane.

Moving along the assembly line, it was dried thoroughly by another diligent employee before I was moved for the third time for the actual cut.

Each procedure was carried out by a different person. It's the Chinese way – a hundred people doing the job of about five in Ireland. The main man, with not a syllable of English, set about clipping me, one hair at a time. It took about half an hour and having not once told anyone what sort of a cut I wanted, due to lack of Mandarin on my behalf and English on his, there was a great sense of anticipation as to the outcome.

Eventually, as if I had done a circular tour of the shop, I was back close to the starting point for a head massage, which sent me to sleep. It was part of the deal. When I woke up, I thought I had been dreaming – until I looked in the mirror to see an image that would have been right at home in an army barracks.

But it was the best haircut of all time – for €3! Now you know why you seldom see a Chinese man with long hair. That night we ended up in an Irish bar playing pool with a few of the Irish team awaiting their flying chariot home including boxer Kenneth Egan – still a bit put out that he didn't win gold.

* * *

'Pulling Like A Dog' In Rio
Eight years later and I arrived in Rio de Janeiro to work at the 2016 games.

Some five hours after they had won their silver medal in rowing, I met the O'Donovan brothers for an interview on the roof of an apartment block overlooking Olympic Park. It was a 10-minute walk away from where RTÉ and the BBC broadcast live links back to studio and was used for its beautiful panoramic backdrop. Do you remember when they did their TV interview pointing behind them trying to convince viewers back home that it wasn't a picture, it was real? I was standing six feet away from them behind the camera understanding what they were trying to say because it did look so unreal.

When they arrived, they looked shattered. They hadn't showered and were still in their racing gear. They hadn't eaten a bit since breakfast, let alone any steaks. So one of our staff ordered pizza, which arrived just after their live "podium pants" interview with Darragh Maloney back in Dublin. They wolfed it down just before Evanne Ní Chuilinn interviewed them again for the nine o'clock news.

It was a great pleasure to meet them and hold the heavy, well-earned silver medals, just them and me and a couple of more colleagues sitting on a Rio rooftop eating pizza, laughing and joking while the country at home celebrated. It was a rare moment of relaxation in those weeks of "pulling like a dog."

I was three weeks there but didn't get to see much of Rio. Hotel, bus, work. Hotel, bus, work. It just didn't feel like the Olympic Games for me. Maybe I was spoiled by the experience and efficiency of Beijing but it was as if we were waiting for these games to begin in earnest and they never really did.

Yes, there were some fantastic performances. One of my favourites was swimmer Katie Ledecky smashing the world record in the 800 metre freestyle final. It was wonderful to be near the finish line in the Olympic stadium on the Thursday night to witness Usain Bolt win the 200 metres. That meant I had been in the stadium live to see Bolt win the 200 in both Beijing and Rio. And of course our own medallists gave us lots to cheer. I was lucky to be the reporter at the sailing for Annalise Murphy's silver medal race and I interviewed her straight afterwards. I watched it in the searing heat on the beach front with her family and friends as they sang The Fields of Athenry in her honour. I had a tight grip of her brother Finn who was jumping and roaring while I tried to interview him live on radio as the waves rolled in around our feet. Quite a surreal scene. Magic, in fact.

But here is the but: the Olympic Games and Rio were uncomfortable bedfellows. There was a sombre edginess in the air with military police and armed guards everywhere you looked. Has it come to this? That we can no longer enjoy what should be happy family sporting events and occasions without the whiff of terror wafting around?

It certainly took from the spirit usually associated with the Olympic Games. The best way I can put it is that the games in Rio were like a square peg in a round hole. Stadiums were unfinished. The livery and logos were skimpy with bare scaffolding instead of colourful entrances.

The Russian drug scandal and Pat Hickey's unseemly arrest didn't help either, casting a long shadow over Rio 2016. It left me somewhat uncomfortable at times knowing that people watching from home just didn't believe in the honesty of the Olympics any more. "Ah, sure he must be on something." Why would I want to be reporting on an event that is false and misleading? Are we being made fools of?

Brazil is a developing country with lots of poverty and more things to worry about than keeping well-off westerners happy. But the language barrier was just that: a barrier and a very frustrating one. Simple things like ordering a coffee or paying a bill became a siege at times. We really are spoiled as an English-speaking country and unfairly we expect others to speak it too. Well, in Brazil, they don't and I got into a tangle a couple of times trying to make basic transactions. Billions were spent on hosting the games while poverty and homelessness remains rife in this city. And at the time, it was being predicted, that the locals would not eventually benefit from it. That is why the lack of warmth of this huge event was evident in Rio. It was a Games that was just about tolerated because despite the city having the honour of being the first in South America to host the Olympics, it was at a huge long-term cost to them as citizens.

* * *

Ring Of Truth On Sport For All Message

I wasn't in London for the 2012 games when Katie Taylor was the Irish hero. In all the jubilation that followed the then junior minister Michael Ring suggested that money be diverted away from our health service and into sport.

While the first part of Michael Ring's quote could be construed in some quarters as risible, there is little doubt about the merits of his next sentence where he said, "the more people that partake in sport, the better." Are the two mutually exclusive?

Paradoxically, a similar viewpoint was proffered in the discussion and debate which followed a not-so positive event, the chaotic Swedish House Mafia concert in the Phoenix Park the same summer. As the post mortem developed into analysing wider social behaviour and personal responsibility, there were plenty of examples given of how teenagers playing sport were less likely to be involved in the sort of violence and hooliganism that went on at that gig.

It would be helpful if we had more scientific analysis of such claims but, anecdotally, if you speak with sports coaches and teachers, they will back up the argument that the young men and women involved in sport in any community are less likely to be hanging around spoiling for trouble.

At one end of the spectrum, boxing coaches will freely tell you that if it wasn't for the local boxing club, many of their members would be sucked into a life of crime. Soccer coaches in areas of high unemployment and social deprivation will equally testify to this. How many of the world's best players would have ended up in jail if it wasn't for soccer, the street game which was the only alternative to delinquency in many ghettos across the globe. At the other end of the sporting spectrum, many of our greatest rugby and GAA players have gone on to become high achievers outside sport. I have no doubt they would be quick to acknowledge the role of sport in their career development.

And then there is the broader community which rides the crest of the sporting wave. The volunteers, supporters, committee members and the proud parents who garner so much joy and no little despair from being joined at the hip with the sport of their choice. There is no denying the physiological and psychological benefits of sport. That is a view from a sports fan. I have no doubt there are plenty who will disagree. All I have to do is devote time on a non-sporting radio programme to sport and texts fly in – "the country is in a mess and all you can talk about is sport...".

The point could be made, the more people we can encourage to take part in sport, the less mess there might be to clean up in future.

*   *   *

Athletics Leaves Other Sports In Its Wake
In my book, the most natural of sports that costs virtually nothing is running. It is also the healthiest, if you run properly and sensibly and avoid injury. I took part in a 5k road race in

the summer of 2017 and I was shocked as I passed kids less than half my age out of breath after only seven or eight minutes of running. They just weren't fit despite the fact that they were still only in their late teens.

I think athletics is the most natural sport there is and arguably the one that requires the most in terms of dedication and sacrifice. You can't teach someone the skill of running in the same way you can teach someone to puck a sliotar, play golf or score a try. Yes, you can be coached in athletics but so much more depends on the individual than in most other sports where there are other forms of support to enhance ability.

In team sports, you can be taken off at half-time and still win. In athletics, if you have an off day, you lose. It's as simple as that.

With sports such as golf and cycling, the more expensive the equipment and technology you use, the more likely you are to succeed. In running, a pair of shoes is the main race-day outlay.

I think Pádraig Harrington is a magnificent sportsman but I shake my head when I hear people suggest that he is Ireland's greatest ever sports star.

Undoubtedly, he has invested thousands of hours into making himself a better golfer and no doubt the sacrifices are huge, but the only comparison I would make between a golfer and an athlete is that they are both on their own, without teammates.

After that I would argue till the cows come home that any Irish athlete who has achieved success on the world stage competing against the best from around the globe on a consistent basis during their career stands heads and shoulders above any major-winning Irish golfer.

For an athlete, it's all about fine-tuning physically and psychologically to the point that once they reach the start line, all that lies between them and success is themselves alone.

Like all elite sportspeople, there must be a talent in the first place but the daily training involved in pushing the body is greatest with an athlete. Once the gun goes, you are totally on your own until the finish line.

Unfortunately, the pressure to succeed has forced some weak athletes to take drugs, which has sullied the name of the sport, but I still won't allow that take from my belief that it is the ultimate sport in terms of endeavour.

*　*　*

Guess Who Brought Tea To China?

I suffered the eternal embarrassment of bringing tea to China when I packed a box of Barry's for my month-long stint at the Beijing Olympics in 2008, much to the amusement of Jimmy Magee. "That's the best I've heard young O'Reilly. You've actually brought tea to China?" he exclaimed, after spotting the red box peering out of my rucksack going from the hotel to IBC one morning. He really got some laugh from that. I forgot to pack any for Rio. It didn't matter, though. Happily for me, as a fairly avid tea-drinker (four or five cups a day), we had a sufficient supply in the RTÉ office at the Olympic Park.

But you know yourself. It's just not the same when it's made with powdered milk. Even the ordinary Brazilian milk made a bad job of the cuppa. It made me appreciate even more the Irish dairy farmer. Having given up coffee about five years earlier, I was left in a quandary, especially on the early mornings when I needed my routine caffeine boost.

So I caved in and began drinking coffee once more on the promise I would climb back on the wagon upon my return home. Somehow I haven't gotten round to it yet and it is driving me bonkers. Because now when I get the urge for a coffee or Americano, it is like a siege as I discovered when I popped into a new trendy café in Dublin city centre soon after returning from Rio. It really took the biscuit when I ordered a sausage roll and a coffee.

The lovely woman at the till handed me the heated sausage roll and a number for delivery of my coffee. OK, I thought, this was a new one on me: getting the hot snack immediately but having to wait for the delayed delivery of my beverage. Well, I had the tasty sausage roll eaten by the time the coffee arrived.

I devoured it while watching the waiter go through the detailed, steamy and quite noisy process of preparing my "tall" Americano, which reminded me of the mission employed by Willy Wonka to make one of those little magic sweets. Banging. Steaming. Battering. Boiling. Dribbling.

After what seemed like an eternity, eventually my long-awaited cup of coffee was brought to me. I am sorry but these cafés are getting worse. The more banging and hammering and steaming and boiling, the swankier the coffee, it seems. You wouldn't hear the likes of it in an aviation service depot.

For heaven's sake, could someone not invent a quieter, quicker way of making a cup of coffee and give all our ears a rest? It's enough to drive a man to, eh, tea.

* * *

Goodbye to Game Of Lousy Frustrations

A noisy coffee machine? Ah yes, I must be getting old because

I am getting grumpy. It doesn't take much though. "You lifted your head," was the advice of my playing partner. As I finished my swing, he was lucky I didn't lift his, clean off his shoulders! It took 15 years of frustration and scuffing the golf ball around the place to realise the sport of the Royal & Ancient and me were not compatible.

I come from a family of golfers who all enjoy the rigmarole and etiquette which comes with the game. Once, while my mother was lady captain at our local golf club, I went out for a summer's evening round of nine holes with her. Behind us, a group of three burly pot-bellied gentlemen decided to give us a gentle reminder to hurry up by teeing off just as we were about to address our balls for our second shots.

My immediate reaction was to turn around and whip the ball back at them, which I did with amazing precision (I can still see them ducking). My mother nearly had a heart attack, considering the prestige of her position within the club, but it was an incident which didn't make the agenda of the next meeting – although it was an early indication of where my golfing career was going.

I just never had the patience for the bluster which came with a round of golf: playing partners of equally moderate ability telling you what you did right or wrong; patronising players who went overboard with the congratulatory comments ("That's your best shot today"). Such blathering frustrated me, especially when the person concerned would be better served keeping their mouths shut.

And then of course there are the television golfers. These fellas are about as useful as a chocolate teapot: multiple practice swings; throwing grass in the air to gauge the wind speed; dressed in the best gear thinking they are being filmed on Sky Sports but are barely able to hit the ball out of their way. Playing with one of them lads can be quite off-putting, especially when one's etiquette threshold is quite low.

Not that I should be laughing. After giving in to a series of lessons, I decided to try to put what I had learned into practice one evening with my dad and my brother. I felt like a robot that had been assembled inside out as I stood up to address the ball. It would have been easier to learn portions of Ulysses by heart. I tried to remember to stand this way, that way and every other way before swinging. After three holes of going steadily backwards, playing worse than ever, I'd had enough. I am embarrassed to admit that I snapped and began bending my clubs over my knee while my brother and father, like trained negotiators at a siege, politely pleaded with me to refrain, afraid anyone at the club would witness this unseemly spectacle.

Eventually, after bending two clubs and realising they wouldn't fit back into my bag, I stormed off, drove home, took the clubs from the boot and threw them against the garden wall, promising never to use them again. And I have stuck to that promise ever since.

*   *   *

Roy Right On Changing Attitude To Winning

Speaking of red mist brings me to Roy Keane, one of my all time sporting heroes. I grew up supporting Manchester United and remember clearly the day he signed for the club for a then record £3.75m in 1993, small beer today. Then there was Saipan nine years later and the rows we all became embroiled in with those who hated him.

And it is an argument which continued for over a decade afterwards. In June 2012 at the European Championship finals, Keane had a pop at Irish fans when he said: "Let's change that attitude towards Irish supporters. Listen, they want to see the team winning as well. Let's not kid ourselves. We're a small country and we're up against it. Let's not go along for the sing-song every now and again".

If we take away Keane's name from that quote, I doubt if there is an Irish supporter who would have disagreed with its sentiments. But because it was Roy Keane, the quote was twisted and spun to whip up the old Saipan civil war again. This was, of course, before Martin O'Neill appointed him as his assistant manager to the Irish team. Both would succeed Giovanni Trappattoni who was boss at that tournament in 2012.

Keane was speaking on ITV to a British audience. He said as an Irish follower he was "flat and disappointed" when asked for his immediate reaction to Ireland's mauling at the hands of Spain during those Euro finals in Poland/Ukraine.

And then he attempted to prove to that audience that Irish supporters are not just a crowd of happy clappy drunks who go to matches and tournaments mainly for the fun and craic, that they do actually have a genuine interest in the football.

That's how I interpreted his remarks and I thought fair play Roy for debunking the stereotype of all Irish fans being flag-waving, beer-guzzling innocents just out for a good time regardless of results.

Back in 2002, I think it is fair to say that Keane's biggest sin in the eyes of so many Irish people, who were more against him than necessarily for McCarthy, was that he played with Manchester United. If you are Irish and you don't follow Manchester United, then you hate them and all belonging to them. When Saipan happened, I argued with ABU friends that they had been waiting in the long grass for Keane. He didn't do international friendlies, meanwhile he was leading Manchester United to Premier League titles and other trophies with pride and passion. It must have stuck in their craw. He seemed more loyal to his club than his country. The reality was lost on them that this was the case with most international stars at big clubs around this time.

Bar one or two exceptions, my anecdotal memory of the Saipan civil war of 2002 was simple. If you were Irish and a Manchester United supporter, then you backed Keane's criticism of the FAI and understood what happened as him being "sent home" by Mick McCarthy. If you were Irish and not a Manchester United supporter, then your read of it was that he never wanted to be there in the first place and had walked out on his team mates and his country. Meanwhile a backhanded compliment from the deluded and the uninformed came in the form of the suggestion that we would have won the world cup had he stayed.

I would argue even to this day that had he played with any other club back then, in particular Liverpool or Celtic, the divide would not have been so great. The ABU mentality kicks in whenever Roy Keane says anything that could be twisted and spun to make him look like he hates his native country – even if it could equally be perceived back in 2012 as him standing up for his fellow countrymen and women.

And that is what happened here. Whether it's Cheltenham week or the Euro finals in Poland, there is a stereotype of the drunk Paddy not giving a fiddlers about anything except having a good time, singing a few bars of a song and drinking lots of porter.

The bellowing of The Fields of Athenry, for the last 10 minutes of the humiliation in Gdansk by men with facepaint played perfectly into that stereotype. I am not a sing-song sort of supporter myself. Quite unusually I prefer to actually watch a match when I go to one. I don't think it's possible to sing and watch a match simultaneously.

Fair play to the Irish fans for singing. I am always moved by their pride. It beats booing, fighting or tearing up the stadium. But what was so wrong with making it clear to a foreign audience that while we are lovely, friendly, harmless people, we do care when our team performs pathetically on the international stage and we do get disappointed when we lose?

Now that Keane is back in the Irish fold, he surely has redeemed his reputation with some, but I'm sure he will never be able to win over others no matter what he does.

Mental Health

Our Dealing With Anxiety And Depression

I remember an incident from about the mid-1990s shortly after I had started working on local radio.

I got a threatening phone call from a gentleman following an interview I had conducted. I was just out of college, had to carry a huge responsibility in the newsroom and had little or no back-up in the form or producers/editors or on site lawyers like RTÉ or most other big media organisations. A horrible feeling engulfed me as he shouted down the phone: "I'm going to sue you and sue your station and you will never work again." This was delivered slowly and menacingly in a Northern accent. It sticks with me even to this day.

The issue was quickly dealt with and the earth continued to spin on its axis. There would be no suing or court case or losing my job. However, for the remainder of the day, the feeling of shock made it feel like a pause button had been pressed in my head.

It gradually faded after a few days but not fully. Indeed for months after, this profound feeling of shock would descend indiscriminately like a dark blanket almost daily. Think about how you felt when you got shocking news of the death of a relative. Now think about enjoying a cup of tea and suddenly getting that feeling without actually hearing any bad news.

It was as if a glass crucible would descend over your body leaving the sounds and colour of the outside world virtually muffled and grey. It would disappear over a period of an hour or so, but I couldn't beat it and hadn't a clue where it was coming from or why.

Then I stumbled across a practical book on how the mind works in mysterious ways. It was a relief to actually read this because, for the life of me, I could not understand how this horrible shock feeling could linger. It was as if the book by Australian health guru Dr. Claire Weekes was written especially for what was happening to me.

I realised that the initial radio station incident was the first time I had experienced any form of "grief" in my life. It unleashed a pow of adrenalin which enjoyed its new-found freedom, swirling around, so much so that it would go to work on me whenever it wanted to. Thanks to Dr. Weekes, now I had found the key to shoehorn this particular genie back into the bottle. It had become totally disproportionate to the original incident which was a sure sign of the onset of something sinister.

To all intents and purposes, I was developing some form of anxiety or mild depression without actually realising it. I didn't need any professional help; instead, I was able to take control and it didn't become an issue again, fizzling out over time. In subsequent years I would hear of performers, be they singers, comedians, actors or journalists and broadcasters (we all loosely fall under the same heading of entertainment) being particularly prone to anxiety and depression. It must have something to do with being at the mercy of the public in a very public way and the pressure to be original, new, and relevant, day after day, week after week. But anxiety, depression and other forms of mental health are not exclusive to the performing arts. It is an indiscriminate condition across the board.

We need a better understanding of the science post trauma, which sow the seeds for mental illness to run riot, rather than focusing on the more simplistic question of why. And I am glad to say from my own relatively innocuous experience, once I focused early on the battle going on in my mind rather than the reason behind it, that glass crucible lifted and stayed lifted. And the tens of thousands of people in Ireland who find themselves in a similar crucible should know that.

*   *   *

Al Delivers A 'New Normal' Line

The young Irish comedian, Al Porter, received a lot of kudos for declaring on The Cutting Edge on RTÉ 1 television in November 2016 that he was on antidepressants. It was an unlikely juxtaposition. Here we had an outwardly carefree, funny man telling the country of a dark state of mind. Of depression. Twitter went into overdrive with tweets of support and sympathy. My reaction? So what?

That is not a cold, callous reaction. It is actually a good thing and here is why: had Al Porter said this three or four years ago, I probably would have joined in the chorus of support (I'm not saying I don't support him).

But now, in my mind anyway, admitting to having a mental illness is finally becoming a new normal.

I met an old friend for a pint some weeks after that. During the course of the night, he made brief reference to the fact that he had gone through "a bit of a depression-type thing". So what? He might as well have told me that he'd had a broken toe which kept him out of playing five-a-side football for a few months.

The strain on the mind of any comedian, to continue oiling the brain's assembly line of new material must be immense and

I would say that a lot of entertainers do succumb to bouts of depression and mental illness as a result.

In the same way that the stresses and worries of daily life affect the rest of us – whether it's about money, our children's health and wellbeing, work or the general uncertainty of the modern world – our mental health is always being pushed to the limit.

Just as some of us are physically better equipped to take a belt, there are some who can withstand mental pressure better than others. So what?

And we shouldn't be afraid to show our emotions. In the summer of 2014, I was sitting on a plane travelling to the United States when I began to cry. I was watching the movie Captain Phillips, a compelling piece of work starring Tom Hanks, arguably the best actor in the world. Towards the end of the movie when he is rescued, the emotional relief he shows is truly spellbinding. That's what got me. I got up from my seat and went to the bathroom to wipe away my tears. You can just imagine how I tried to be discreet in front of other passengers. I didn't want them to see me crying. I am a man, after all. And men don't cry, do they? Well the answer is we do and we should not be afraid to cry more.

We should not be afraid to show our emotions in times of crisis, sadness, elation or happiness. Ironically, when I returned to my seat, I read an interview with my old pal Seán Bán Breathnach. SBB famously cried while commentating on Katie Taylor's Olympic final success. And in the interview, he referred to this and how he is inclined to cry more or less at the drop of a hat. It made me feel a little bit better, that it is okay to be a grown man and openly show emotion like this.

Soccer pundit Johnny Giles doesn't agree. He has derided

Premier League players like John Terry and Luis Suarez for crying on TV, suggesting that it was a sort of fashion statement playing to the cameras and that it didn't happen in his day. Of course, it didn't happen in his day. Men of the 20th century didn't cry. It was a sure sign of weakness. Has anyone ever seen their dad cry, for instance? Not many, I'd say. Quite what Giles made of his sparring partner Eamon Dunphy crying some time back on The Late Late Show, I am not sure. If memory serves me right, Dunphy's tears were brought on by a discussion about the recession. And indeed the recession has given reason for many of us to cry and be emotional. But how many men in particular are hurting inside, afraid to let go of the emotion and stress of losing a job or not being able to pay the mortgage? And what is that clamming up doing to their minds in the long run? It surely cannot be good to clam up.

In these tough times when suicide particularly among young men is such a problem in this country, men should be encouraged to open up about their inner feelings. Emotional torment should not be suppressed and it shouldn't be seen as a sign of weakness or vulnerability for a man to turn to his wife or his family and release any inner feelings of sadness or distress. Yet my immediate reaction to the tears streaming down my face 35,000 feet in the air was: "Oh gosh, I hope nobody can see me."

It's not the first time that I have shed tears as a grown man. I have had many reasons to be emotional over the years. And I am singling out men here because women are way ahead of us in dealing and coping with pressure and emotion.

Women are more inclined to talk to others about their problems and stresses. As I said earlier, it's unlikely that most of us have seen our dads cry but likely that we have seen our mothers or our sisters cry.

It's time that we accepted that us men have emotions too and we shouldn't be afraid to show them.

* * *

Why Do We Forget Names?

I worry about it a little at times. But comfortingly others worry about it too. Forgetfulness and, in particular, forgetting names. It is the ultimate embarrassment to meet someone on the street and forget their name. I've become a master at scrambling about in my mind to fill the conversational void, silently racing through the alphabet for any clue as to who on earth I am chatting to.

Meantime, understandably, the ire of my forgotten subject rises in indignation at my apparent aloofness. I'd be annoyed if the shoe was on the other foot. Because, in Ireland, if you don't greet an acquaintance by name, it is seen as, well, ignorant, as I'm not of the "hi, how are you" generation. Many times I have faced this pickle of taking longer than normal to bolt on a name to the generic greeting of: "How are you doing?"

There are two types of forgetting names. Whatever about being approached by a relative stranger whom I wouldn't necessarily be expected to know as they reintroduce themselves three or four years after our last meeting at a wedding or in a radio studio, getting a blank as a work acquaintance or a near neighbour cheerily approaches out of context worries me when it happens.

One time a few years ago (I can't remember exactly when) I arrived on a farm to record an interview and the farmer had a great welcome for me. Nothing unusual there, except that he welcomed me back to the farm.

For the life of me I could not remember the last time I was there. Fair enough, I have been to hundreds of farms over the years, but, up until that point, I am sure I would never visit one for the second time only for me to believe it to be my maiden visit.

I played along so as not to offend, looking out for some landmark that would jog my memory. It would be funny if it wasn't true. Then I heard Ruby Wax on RTÉ's Radio 1 one morning. She has just written a book called 'A mindfulness guide for the frazzled.' It resonated.

"The first thing that goes when you are in a state of high anxiety is your memory," she told Ryan Tubridy. Aha! So, I am in a high state of anxiety and stress. Is that what is causing these momentary lapses in memory?

I am not so sure.

But she did make some valid points about the world we live in and the way we are bombarded with information and people and happenings from the minute we get up until we try to slow the brain down at night. The mind can only take so much.

Whatever about getting older and conditions such as dementia, I put my episodes down to a lack of concentration and maybe laziness. I should live in the moment more. I am often introduced to people and 10 seconds later I forget their names. That isn't a medical condition. It's called not concentrating and most of us do it.

Anyway, I now realise that training the brain is as important in midlife as training the body. Now, where did I leave my cup of tea...?

* * *

Speaking Up For The Common Good

Speaking of remembering, 'Telltale-tattler, buy a ...' I bet everyone could finish that childhood rhyme off. We were brought up hearing that in the schoolyard. If you told the teacher on someone, you were a telltale. In secondary school, the offender became a snitch, while in a more sinister world, the telltale would have become known as a grass or an informer.

The more modern whitecollar term is what is now commonly referred to as a whistle-blower and has only entered the national lexicon relatively recently. What was the whistle-blower called before that? A snitch? A grass? A telltale?

Whatever the name, nobody had any time for someone "ratting" on someone else. To avoid hassle of such an accusation during my school days, I kept the head down and steered clear the best I could from situations which would have compromised my wishes to live a peaceful life. Minding your own business could be deemed as another antidote to running the risk of being a rat.

Maybe that is why I never had the sort of mind to go marching or protesting. Is this related to having a profound fear of speaking out, a manifestation of growing up petrified of being labelled a snitch, a grass, a telltale? Or maybe it is in reality that bizarre social shyness I have. But you can call me weak if you wish.

The demonising of the school telltale from a young age spawned a routine of minding one's own business. Consequently – and demonstrably in our recent history – this paved the way for bully boys and bully-boy politics to prosper. Turning our collective heads the other way has always been the easiest option. The instinct was to keep your mouth shut if you saw anything untoward, be it in the schoolyard, your neighbour's house, in work or even at home. We can go back to the abuse by priests, teachers and coaches of little children and how heads turned the other way. "Don't be telling tales."

That all changed in the 1990s with the unmasking of paedophiles across a range of professions, most notably in education, in the church, and of course in the family home.

But even then, remember how sections of society reacted to the victims as a result of our ingrained despising of the telltale, even if it was against the monstrosity of paedophilia? There were those still willing to label the victims as being somewhat inferior.

Despite the emergence in this new era of people no longer being afraid to highlight wrongdoing, the telltale stigma remains. It is probably demeaning to make this glib comparison considering the seriousness of what they highlight but the whistle-blower has become a celebrated figure, particularly in the financial services and health sectors. But the old schoolyard attitude hasn't changed in An Garda Síochána it seems, where highlighting injustice, malpractice and wrongdoing is still frowned upon among some of its number. Therein surely lies an irony.

Yes, the salt-of-the-earth Dublin street traders and the women who ran the household on small country farms had more in common than they realised

The Irish Mammy

Is It Mam, Mammy Or Mummy?

For me, it's Mam, not Mum; Mammy, not Mummy. I could never get this Mum or Mummy business. Maybe it's a cultural divide. The kids in school with country parents referred to their Mammy. The rest around places like Castleknock spoke of Mum or Mummy. The Americanisation of the Irish dialect was taking hold as far back as the '80s or did Irish Mums exist before colour television?

There are also pockets of Dublin where Mammy reigns supreme, like near where Mrs Brown reared her boys. Yes, the salt-of-the-earth Dublin street traders and the women who ran the household on small country farms had more in common than they realised. They reared big families and they were Mammies, not Mummies.

Mammy is as patently Irish as "you're grand", and I am trying but failing to imagine the offspring of any other English speaking nation referring to their Mammy. So why do we have to go all Mom and Mum?

Then there is mother. The more refined, the landed referred to "mother." There is an air of reverence to it, a real show of respect if you referred to "mother." I always conjure up the image of a matriarch, a true champion of the home, the real boss, whenever what I would refer to as "mammy" was and is referred to as "mother." I like it but I would have been too ordinary to shout "mother when looking for my school tie, too country to yell "mummy."

And what about ma? As in: "Me Ma is calling me for me

dinner." This was a somewhat uniquely pubescent Dublin term of endearment, where my Mammy became me Ma at around 13 years of age. I don't think Mummy became me ma though from memory.

Sadly, Mammies and Mam's are a dying species, if the Mother's Day cards are anything to go by. I would defy you to find a Mother's Day card for your Mammy. Lots of Mummies and Mums but few Mammies and Mams. It's the same with Christmas and birthday cards.

Anyway, regardless of how you refer to her, it's all the same. We only have one and we are the lesser without them.

* * *

They're All Out Of Step...

Mammies don't like hearing criticism of their children from TV sports pundits. A few years ago we were discussing some issue related to TV punditry on RTÉ Radio's *Liveline* when the mother of a prominent Dublin county footballer rang up out of the blue to complain about how upsetting it was to read newspaper articles which were critical of her son.

Obviously, she didn't name him and we gave her a pseudonym to protect her anonymity. She let fly, naming one pundit in particular who had written a critical piece about her son. It was, what we call in the business, radio gold. The named pundit happened to be a good friend of mine and immediately after the programme he rang me chuckling.

Mercifully, it wasn't his solicitor ringing to complain that his client had been libelled by a fuming woman on national radio. From her comments, he was able to decipher the player in question. Contrary to the mother's strong-held theory of victimhood, this former player had no vendetta but had merely pointed to her son's shortcomings in the course of his analysis of the Dublin team. Nevertheless, there's nothing like a mother scorned. He had gotten on the wrong side of the wrong mammy.

Separately, I once heard the great Dublin forward, Bernard Brogan, refer to how his own mother gets very annoyed when she hears or reads criticism of her boys. And it's understandable that a parent would get upset to hear their child being criticised in public, regardless of their superstar status. Being paid well might soften the blow, I suppose, if you are Mammy McIlroy.

*   *   *

Thank God For Pat And Joe

Each summer Joe Brolly and Pat Spillane become hate figures across Ireland. How silly considering the alternative – interviews and analysis from current players and managers. My God, the clichéd drivel they come out with is a definite cure for insomnia. If I had my way – and I have said it to my radio sport colleagues who have the misfortune of conducting the excruciating pre- and post-match interviews – I wouldn't broadcast as much as a syllable from any player or manager during the football and hurling championships. They just play everything down, talk up the opposition and give the impression that they don't really have a hope on Sunday. Then when the match is over they have the temerity to blast all the pundits who "didn't give us a chance". "We knew from the start that we were going to win this championship".

Well, why didn't you say that before the match? So, thank God for Joe Brolly, Pat Spillane et al for bringing some life, sense and colour to the banal mutterings of monotone managers and players who obviously would rather stick needles in their eyes than talk to their fans and supporters via radio or TV. You know what? Maybe we should interview their Mammies instead.

*   *   *

Staunch hurling people have a good way of rising other more passive observers with the hoary old argument that theirs is the greatest game in the world. It's a totally subjective argument. You are never going to convince a soccer man that "stick fighting" is better than his sport, no more than you are going to satisfy a hurling man that the "beautiful game" is more beautiful. I stay out of it, although I find it hard to concentrate the mind on a Premier League match directly after watching a good hurling game.

But while hurling is celebrated for its brilliance and its unique Irishness, there are large swathes of this small country that haven't seen a ball pucked in anger, or at least not on a regular or semi-competitive basis, for ages. Less than half the counties on the island actually compete in the All-Ireland senior championship. So what does that say about the GAA that, despite all its parochial power, it has failed after 130 years to give this spectacular sport a foothold in many parts of the country?

Here are arguably three reasons why this is the case. Firstly, population. Clubs and, by extension, counties are just too small to fish out of the same talent pool. Cork, maybe Dublin and Galway to a lesser extent, are the only counties with relatively strong football and hurling teams deemed capable of competing equally for provincial honours. That brings us on to the second reason – tradition. No matter what you do, you are not going to coax a Cavan football man to push hurling in his local GAA club in the same way a Kilkenny hurling man will never encourage his son to play football first. And, finally hassle. I see it among young kids. It's more difficult to hone the skills of hurling and, given the choice, nine- and 10-year olds, particularly in dual clubs, will throw the hurley, helmet and sliotar to one side and opt for the more straightforward game of football instead.

* * *

Not Scoring During Mick Interview

Anyway back to the awkwardness of the sporting interview. I remember many years ago, on a wet winter night I found myself interviewing Irish soccer manager Mick McCarthy at Gortakeegan, the home of Monaghan United Football Club. He was a guest of the club at the unveiling of a new stand built through proceeds raised by its supporters' club. My first question was along the lines of: "Mick, isn't the building of this stand a fine achievement for such a small soccer club?"

He looked at me maddeningly before spurting back: "Where I come from, we call it a football club, alright?" The interview didn't last too long as I immediately lost what little interest I had.

Mick had done a thousand press interviews in his career and probably has a natural scepticism about journalism as a profession. And who could blame him when you consider some of the stuff that was written about him by the tabloids.

But here I was doing my job, asking a soft but relevant question, having being invited to do the interview by the club, who were looking for publicity. I thought it only polite to have the Irish manager swell their heads by offering his approval of their great endeavour in answering such a question.

 But I felt he looked down on me as a reporter, and made it look as if I didn't know my "soccer" from my "football." What he didn't know was that my listeners had virtually no interest in the trials and tribulations of the now defunct Monaghan United, despite the many fine men that put their heart and soul into running the club. He also wouldn't have known how they winced at his condescending interview in the face of them trying to entice new fans in the gate.

Recently Jim Gavin had a lash at RTÉ over the broadcasters coverage of the Diarmuid Connolly altercation with a linesman in Dublin's 2017 championship match with Carlow. Mickey Harte has refused for many years to speak with RTÉ. That is to do with a much more personal issue. Davy Fitzgerald also had a go at hurling analyst Michael Duignan following Wexford's defeat to Waterford also in the 2017 hurling championship. And some time back I remember Kildare manager Kieran McGeeney having a lash at pundits in the days following Kildare's exit from the All-Ireland football championship, branding one or all as cowards.

Banality has become the default setting for many of our GAA stars when confronted with a microphone. I always reach for the off button when a pre-match interview is queued. Dead air would be more fulfilling. And if I was ever asked to go to a GAA press night, my first question to my boss would be: "What have I done so wrong to deserve this?"

Do managers and players not recognise the irony in their criticisms? Pundits are a necessary invention borne out of the sheer vacuous media space occupied by the modern GAA manager and player. They have absolutely nothing to say. And the more a decent reporter tries to press for an answer which supporters would like to hear answered, the more they reach for the inane.

In rugby and soccer, managers have an obligation to speak to the press. They are so much part of the circle of hype which pays their wages that they know the importance of their role in the whole money-go-round. Obviously GAA managers and players don't benefit in the same financial manner. In all honesty, the media are under a compliment to them.

But they could be a little more adventurous with their comments. It's for the fans after all. Joe Canning's candid interview in a national newspaper 24 hours ahead of the 2017 All Ireland semi-final between Galway and Tipperary in which he scored that mesmerising last-gasp winning point served to prove that managers and players don't have to resort to the vacuous for fear of a kind of negative karma if they do. Loosen up lads, will ye?

*Davy Fitz and
Micheál Donoghue
squaring up along the line as
we jaunted along behind a
tractor hurrying home
the hay before the
next downpour*

Kids Corner

Summer Time – And The Living Is Easy

Tramore. Beach, sand, sun and arcade machines – any child's paradise. Summer 2016 made me wish I was a child again. It's a no-frills spot but it fits the bill if you are aged about seven to 15.

It was near the end of July and just days before I would have to wave bye bye to the family ahead of the three week decamp to Rio. Having absorbed the thrill of the Red Arrows on the Bray seafront at lunchtime, we took off down the spine of the east coast, zigzagging through the three Ws of Wicklow, Wexford and Waterford (with a little bit of Kilkenny sandwiched in between).

It rained but then the sun shone, reminding us that it was indeed summer in Ireland as we listened to the hurling drama from Thurles. Davy Fitz and Micheál Donoghue squaring up along the line as we jaunted along behind a tractor hurrying home the hay before the next downpour.

Ferns. Stop for ice-cream and the ambience of weather, hurling on the radio, slow tractors, round bales and a dripping cone combined to create a summer Sunday afternoon unique to rural Ireland. Timeless. We all remember those summer Sunday drives. And the magic of the seaside.

On a cloudy cool Monday afternoon, following three competitive rounds of crazy golf, as the tide moved out, we dashed into the water up to our waists. What seemed like daylight madness turned into a trick. Jumping salty waves with trousers twisted to above the knee, the awkwardness of having not only soaking trousers but a soaking T-shirt above the naval turned into the best 20 minutes fun you could have on any holiday.

Proud parents are 10 a penny. And I am one of them, particuarly when it comes to their attitude to school. "You can be anybody you want if you stick to the books" is an old fashioned mantra they are sick of hearing from me. But I sighed and they giggled when we played one of these "waiting" games. To pass the time waiting for our hot chocolates outside a café on the prom, I conducted a quiz. I name the town, they name the county. The answers were hilarious. "Where is Ballyshannon?" "Eh, Cork," says one; "Louth!" shouts the other.

What has happened to geography in school, I ask? "It's all stalactites and stalagmites Dad," came the reply. But you can't blame them. When I was their age, I knew every town in every county. I suppose that's because on those summer Sunday drives, we actually drove through these places. And the word SatNav didn't exist. Now you can drive from Belfast to Cork and Dublin to Tramore without seeing a main street, turning routine knowledge of towns and villages into a nerdy pastime.

Still after a fun filled three days enjoying a simple old - fashioned Irish holiday, they won't forget Tramore in a hurry I hope.

* * *

This Is London Calling...
Impulse is a virtue and, despite rather unfavourable currency exchange rates, the BBC theme tune to Wimbledon and a vacuum in the children's busy summer holiday schedule

conspired to make me book a three-day getaway to London the year previous.

We flew into Stansted before jumping on to the express train direct to Liverpool Street, close to where we were staying. I have been to London many times, mainly on short business trips and never long enough to make much use of the underground system. Well, we certainly made up for it on this trip.

We bought Oyster cards, which were a Godsend as we whizzed our way across the city, criss-crossing lines in and out of a myriad of stations, Temple, Bank, Blackfriars, Monument and so on. Soon I left it to Deirbhile and Patrick to do the navigating as we moved around and marvelled at their understanding and enthusiasm for the underground system.

Patrick was like the veritable Japanese tourist, snapping on his little camera all the sights and landmarks. It was effectively an educational holiday as we hit the predictable touristy hotspots, but the pièce de résistance for the little man came when we took the tube to Fulham Broadway for a tour of Stamford Bridge, the home ground of Patrick's beloved Chelsea. It's no Croke Park, I can tell you, but to witness the face of a nine-year-old sports fanatic as he slowly scanned the changing room and dugout, was a sight to behold.

Not to be outdone, for Deirbhile who loves athletics, we scooted out to the Olympic Stadium in east London. Eventually, exhausted, we arrived back into Dublin after a hassle-free, fun-filled three days in a brilliant, bustling city.

From the Olympic stadium, Buckingham Palace, Big Ben, Number Ten and Chelsea, to The London Eye, Westminster Abbey, Tower Bridge and a boat trip along the Thames, I turned to Patrick and asked: "Well, what was your highlight?".

He thought for a moment before replying: "Dad, it was definitely the man on the unicycle in Covent Garden."

* * *

Hidden Secrets Of Croke Park

From Stamford Bridge to Croke Park. There is no comparison. "The Meath team, when managed by Sean Boylan, used to meditate in this warm-up room before matches."

"What? Sean Boylan's teams, some of the hardiest, toughest players ever to play Gaelic football, used to meditate before matches?"

That was one of the many interesting anecdotes I learned about during another day out with the children this time to Croke Park. We weren't there for a match, but, rather, to take the tour of Europe's fourth largest sports arena. It was a wet, dreary Sunday and, looking for something to do, I came up with the bright idea of the tour. We have always tried to make good use of spare time with the children. Whether it's going to see the Book of Kells, visiting Newgrange or spending an afternoon at the Natural History Museum, the children are at the sort of age now where you want to bring them to these educational sites. In a few more years, they will have found new interests as teenagers and probably won't go to these places of their own volition.

Ireland has a rich tapestry of interesting, historical sites, most of which many of us have never visited, yet tourists come specially to see. Unless you have been to the Cliffs of Moher or Clonmacnoise as a youngster, it's less likely that you will take time to visit these places as an adult. But as a child, when you go to see the Book of Kells or visit the Giant's

Causeway, the memory will stick forever.

Now, the few miles of a trip from Castleknock to Croke Park may not seem like the most original or exciting of excursions, but I have seldom enjoyed a tour like this before. It was a real case of going in with little or no expectation and coming away very pleased. On arrival at the impressive museum, we watched a fly-on-the-wall documentary about a day in the life of Croke Park.

Did you know that there are 10,000 seats in Croke Park which the GAA have to actually rent from the railway authorities for each match because, technically, the seats are outside the boundary line of Croke Park, encroaching on-high into private property beside the railway line? Did you know that the huge million euro screen situated where the old Nally Stand once stood is the largest outdoor screen in Europe? And did you know that there are 32 steps up to the presentation area in the Hogan Stand to signify that the winning captain has walked across thirty one other counties to reach the summit? We were bamboozled with lots of interesting, historical and anecdotal facts. Rubble from the 1916 Rising remains underneath the renovated Hill 16, which, of course, is named after the Rising.

In the dressing room area we found out that even though Croke Park is a national stadium, Dublin almost always use the same dressing room, except when they played Armagh. Why? Well, the dressing rooms, one and two, are allocated in alphabetical order as Gaeilge.

In the warm-up area we were also told that Tyrone manager Mickey Harte places a punch bag in the centre of the arena with the opposition jersey squeezed over it. You can guess the rest. We were also taken pitch side and up to the press area with which, of course, I am familiar. And, finally we went to the museum where, among many things, we spent time developing our shooting skills. It was two hours well spent.

* * *

Bright Boots And Mohicans

Far be it from me to focus on the nuances of today's sports commentators, but how the lexicon has changed from when I was a young fella. I was kicking a ball around on the green beside my parents' house with Patrick when I was brought back to my youth playing on the same green. I had just bought my boy a new pair of football boots, or "Neymars", as he calls them, in tribute to the star Brazil striker. They were bright orange with a dash of luminous yellow. The players endorsing these must earn a fortune for wearing them judging by the impulsiveness of young wannabe footballers like Patrick.

Whatever about the boots, I began to get worried watching a match on TV during the 2014 World Cup when he compared the haircuts of these superstars, designed especially for the global TV audience. Next morning, before his hurling match, he was looking for hair gel. Parents, be prepared – this is the future: bright boots and Mohicans.

Anyway, he wore the Neymars to a hurling match the following Saturday, so I didn't need to use the colour of his helmet to identify him through the scrum of a typical crowded-around the-ball under-8s match. He glowed, physically and metaphorically of course – and he scored the winning goal against the local rivals. I was just relieved that he didn't do a Neymar style celebration. Whatever about the boots, it's not the GAA way to celebrate like Neymar. We prefer the Joe

Canning style of getting on with it, as he did after his amazing point salvaged a draw against Kilkenny 24 hours later.

When I was Patrick's age, my first boots were a simple pair of black Golas with three luminous green stripes down the side. The laces were so long you wrapped them several times around the bottom of the boot. They went beautifully with my replica O'Neill's Ireland strip, the jersey with a texture which probably could allow you stretch it around Croke Park three or four times. That's what I was wearing when playing on the green beside my mother's house doing mock commentaries of our greatness.

Those were the days when you used to play to win a match. Now, you play to get "a result". Back then, a poor goalkeeper might let the ball fall, but today's commentators call that "spilling the ball". Players today "press the ball", "boss the midfield", "stretch the back four", "put their foot through the ball", "push forward", "put their head on the ball" and "ask questions of the opposition".

Back on the green in the '80s, there was no stoppage time – we just kept playing until someone was called for dinner. We played hurling without helmets too, although it's only right that all hurlers must wear helmets nowadays. The only problem is that inter-county hurling heroes are less recognisable in their street clothes.

Perhaps it's why the likes of Neymar with his mad haircut and crazy boots is more identifiable to young fans than Joe Canning. Maybe luminous orange helmets are the way to go.

* * *

Counting The Tweets For Science

"So, what are we doing today Dad?" Patrick is a great man for keeping me on my toes. Every weekend requires planning. It's a good way to be. The alternative is to do nothing and I always say that in a few years, the children will be doing their own thing and won't want to be out with their parents.

"I have passes for the Young Scientist Exhibition."

"Yes," was his enthusiastic response. It was the last day of the exhibition and a bit like the last day of the Ploughing, the fatigue was showing a little on the faces of the hundreds of young exhibitors who had been there three days. Nevertheless, it was so brilliantly interesting that we would have put in several hours more.

I don't want to sound patronising but what I enjoyed most was the polite and mannerly way in which the youngsters engaged with us big adults. It was lovely to observe Patrick's interaction with the students too. In the primary school section, two sixth class girls confidently approached us, introduced themselves and asked if we would like to visit their stand, where they were presenting the results of a survey on the use of social media in Ireland. They made it really interesting by asking Patrick and I multiple-choice questions.

"How many tweets are sent every minute?"

"How many people log on to Facebook in Ireland each day?"

The irony is that if we weren't at the RDS, we probably would have been slouched at home adding to that number staring into our phones.

As we left, feeling very fulfilled that we had invested quality time into something very worthwhile and very educational, I said to Patrick that the lesson I learned from the day was how it is always good to be polite and engaging with people, not to be shy or dismissive. It is a lovely trait in a young person if they engage and be chatty – particularly with adults. It is also a valuable tool in helping a young person to get on in life.

Being polite and inquisitive in this way can build confidence.

And it is a quality which all of these students possessed and I was chuffed that we were able to absorb all of this. Then we sat into the car. I switched on the radio to listen to the sport and Patrick put on his headphones to watch Top Gear on his iPod.

*   *   *

In Dublin's Fair City

Living close to Dublin city, we are lucky we do things on impulse. The experience of the Young Scientist Exhibition was an enjoyable one but they aren't always so joyous and colourful.

"Let's jump on the train and go into town." Good plan. With nothing else on the agenda one dull autumn Saturday, we headed into the city centre for an afternoon walkabout.

We got off the train at Pearse St Station and rambled around to The Farm restaurant (where else) on Dawson St for a lovely lunch. As we left to dodge the crowds towards Grafton St, wrapped up warm with our bellies full, a sense of guilt came over me as we tripped across several homeless people, slouched and dotted along the side of the footpath, battered coffee cups held out looking for anything anyone could spare.

Now, I am easily taken in at the best of times. Charity collectors always hit the jackpot when they knock on my door. You could say it's a nice attribute to possess but the line between being generous and being a fool is very thin. When a tin is rattled in front of me, outside mass or at the local shopping centre, my money and I are easily parted. That's the fool in me, even if it's for a good cause.

But I would like to think that what tugged at my heart that Saturday was a genuine feeling of sadness at the plight of all of these people begging for a living. How can people not have some sympathy, even anger about it? And it also allowed my children to see and learn, first-hand, that life is not all a bed of roses. I made a point of stopping to give these people what change I could, trying my best to decipher the chancers from the genuinely needy.

On spotting one poor man shivering with a lifeless look on his face, I bought him a cup of coffee and a banana. It just felt like the right thing to do and I could see he really appreciated it. Even the elderly lady, well-dressed and hidden along a side street playing the accordion, or the tiny little girl standing in a shop doorway playing the violin with her older sister standing a few feet away keeping an eye, gave me a lump in my throat.

Maybe this is their hobby, playing music on the street, but it's more likely they need this money to survive. I found that hard to accept even though it was a new reality for people struck down by our near decade of recession.

As we passed the time until our return train home to Castleknock, Deirbhile wanted to visit the GPO as she had never been inside it before. Outside, there were three men standing at a table giving out leaflets about becoming a Muslim. Just around the corner on Henry St, an African man with a loud hailer screeched that if we did not believe in God, we would be punished and sent to hell.

As we turned and crossed over by the Spire to the other side of O'Connell St, an elderly man dressed all in black bellowed that if we did not believe Jesus Christ was the son of God, then we are all liars.

"Why is he saying that?" asked Patrick, a little intimidated. His older sister tried to defuse his fear, suggesting it was an act. And maybe she is right. But as we walked on towards Connolly Station, I thought to myself if they were really caring, they'd throw away their leaflets and loud hailers, stop frightening people with their preaching and go help their fellow human beings shivering on the nearby streets, who must wonder through their pain if there really is a Jesus, a God, an Allah or whatever.

*When we landed in Liege,
I switched on my phone and
noticed a missed call from
home. Something was up!*

Terror Attacks

Finding Myself In The Middle Of Brussels Blasts

We were about to descend to the airport. The captain had indicated some time before that we were "10 minutes to landing". Then almost unbeknownst to us all, the plane began rising slowly. The captain came back on: "Brussels air traffic control has informed us that the airport is closed and we are diverting to Liege."

That was March 22, 2016, the morning terrorists bombed Brussels. I was heading for the Forum for the Future of Agriculture. Usually I fly there the night before and get the metro from Maelbeek station to cover the short journey to the venue called The Square close to the centre of Brussels, which hosts this annual event. But the cost of flying in on a Monday night was prohibitively expensive, hence the early Tuesday arrival. That morning before leaving Dublin, I'd heard on the news about another French air traffic control disruption. They are common and cause chaos. I thought to myself that in some roundabout way, this was the reason Brussels was now closed. I cursed them under my breath as we ascended into the sky again. I was going to miss the important opening session of the conference. A wasted journey.

When we landed in Liege, I switched on my phone and noticed a missed call from home. Something was up. Then everyone on the plane began to check their phones and iPads to see what had happened. Brussels Airport had been bombed by terrorists, most likely Isis. After about half an hour sitting on the runway in Liege the captain came on again to inform passengers that those who wished to return to Dublin could stay on the plane. I was now going to miss the entire conference and my arranged meeting with European Commissioner for Agriculture Phil Hogan. I reverted to news-gathering mode.

I was still going to Brussels but not to the Forum for Agriculture, rather to see what I could do for my radio colleagues on other news programmes. It didn't for a split second dawn on me to sit on the plane and go back home. The immediate instinct was journalistic, which was to get to Brussels as fast as I possibly could. My Dad was on the phone. He knew I was going and had woken up to the news on the radio. He was panicking until I returned his call.

The airport in Liege was calmly chaotic, if there is such a thing. There were police dogs and machine guns all over the place while a mobile screening unit for arriving passengers going into the airport was being hastily constructed outside the front of the terminal. I shouted out to a group of Irish who had disembarked if anyone wanted to share a taxi to Brussels. A husband and wife who were there to celebrate their wedding anniversary, and had decided to proceed onwards regardless, agreed to split the fare for the one-hour journey to Brussels rather than wait for a bus transfer which was being promised. The local radio station was broadcasting in Flemish in the taxi but I could almost follow what was being reported. This was like Brussels' 9-11 as army trucks and police cars passed us along the motorway heading west to the capital.

When we arrived in Brussels, I made my way to my hotel in the EU quarter. Once I got past the outer cordon which was being manned by police with guns and balaclavas, the 20 minute walk from where I was dropped off to my hotel was eerily quiet. There was nobody around and no cars allowed in towards the city. So amidst all the chaos and terror, there was actually an air of calm. Always bustling, it was now deserted save for soldiers, police and camera crews. I set about interviewing people around there and in the city centre for various RTÉ radio programmes on Tuesday evening and Wednesday morning. I stood by the sealed-off road outside Maelbeek metro station, which had also been bombed. Exactly two weeks previous, I had been in that metro during morning rush hour in the city. Earlier that year, I had a cup of tea in the Starbucks which was blasted by one of the airport bombers.

When one is so familiar with an area that has been affected like this, it makes what happened all the more shocking, particularly this city which has been crawling with armed soldiers and police for the best part of the previous 12 months. But as one colleague noted, it doesn't matter. If terrorists want to attack, they will attack.

The following day, I returned home via Charleroi Airport as Brussels Airport remained closed. As I sat in the crowded airport, I suddenly remembered that the previous Friday, I was presenting *Drivetime* on RTÉ Radio, standing in for regular presenter, Mary Wilson. The ringleader in the November 2015 Paris attacks Salah Abdeslam had finally been captured in Brussels after four months on the run and I did an interview about his arrest with a Brussels-based reporter. As the programme finished, I half-jokingly remarked to the programme producer Tom Donnelly that I was going to Brusssels the following Tuesday and would be there if there was a terror attack or words to that effect. Little did I think it would actually turn out that way as I stood that Tuesday evening beside the metro station close to the iconic Berlaymont building reporting events back to Mary Wilson in studio.

*   *   *

Searching For Peace With An Invisible Enemy

When the IRA was killing innocent people with their guns and bombs in Northern Ireland and England throughout the 1970s, 80s and 90s, there was always the hope that it would end through negotiation. There was a political channel from Westminster to the Army Council via Sinn Féin. It took nearly 30 years and much bloodshed, but eventually a solution was found. Their aim? Brits out. It didn't happen but depending on what side you were on, a win had been secured by way of the so-called "peace process".

So likening the Isis suicide bombing in Brussels and other relatively recent attacks around Europe in the likes of Manchester, London, Paris, Berlin and Barcelona with the indiscriminate IRA campaign is somewhat trite. At least the IRA was eventually willing to talk. Their aim, as unrealistic as it was (to think that the British would be bombed out of the North), was at least tangible by other means. With this abomination known as Isis, we have no clue what they really want or how they are to be negotiated with.

In a similar way the debate about the Provisional IRA can be brought back 40 years, 100 years or 800 years, trying to find the trigger of the emergence of Isis can be traced to the failed 2010 Arab Spring or the 2003 invasion of Iraq. Or we can go back centuries if we want to find the source.

I don't see Isis as an army but more as a belief that will be hard to exterminate even if the USA and Russia worked together to do so. To me there are more than enough people willing to carry on its warped ideology. An ideology that has stretched to beyond getting the West out of Middle Eastern affairs. Solving the problem has certainly not been helped by trying to impose a Western type democracy to a culture that is obviously adverse to it.

It is in its more fundamentalist form a warped desire to make us subservient to their ways which are diametrically opposed to Western culture including pop music. In the meantime, the young brainwashed jihadis continue to believe in fantasy. In a world of seven billion people, there are lunatics of all faiths and races with no respect for human life – even their own.

Being able to latch onto a campaign like that of Islamic fundamentalism gives such chilling minds a bit of a kick what with their "virgins in heaven" and Isis is lapping it up. Lunatics with an excuse for their lunacy. In America, the young white male equivalent buys a gun and heads for the local high school. In other words, warped crackpots won over by ridiculous ideology or radicalised by some profound belief exist everywhere regardless of creed or nationality.

In Northern Ireland, there was always the hope that peace would prevail through negotiation. In this instance, who exactly are we to negotiate with and about what specifically?

* * *

Migrants And The Importance Of Integration

I was chatting to a taxi driver in Berlin during Euro 2016 and I asked him about Germany's hopes in the semi-final the following night. He told me that he didn't care, that he was Turkish.

He was born and bred in Germany but he was Turkish. His parents were Turkish and his friends are Turkish, and they all follow Turkey. He lives in Germany and works in Germany but didn't hide his disdain for all things German.

I am sure there are many London taxi drivers with cockney accents who consider themselves Irish, sing Irish songs and follow Irish teams courtesy of one or both of their parents having crossed the Irish sea. But this was different. My Berliner driver showed a complete indifference to the country that was his home. And therein lies a big problem across pockets of Europe: a lack of integration which is breeding the sort of hate in Parisian and Brussels suburbs and has created some of the nutcases masquerading as fighters under the abhorrence that is Isis.

Earlier in the year, I drove through the now infamous Molenbeek neighbourhood in Brussels. Dilapidated, there were no western faces but exclusively middle eastern and north African looking men, mostly in Arabic dress, sitting on kerbs and standing on street corners kicking their heels.

In London and Paris too, there are examples of areas totally populated by immigrant communities with little sign of the culture of the country they inhabit. Is it that these communities blatantly don't want to be part of their host country or is it that they feel unwelcome as outsiders? Either way, it's unhealthy to the point that it has bred and is breeding a hatred of western culture and western men, women and children. It works both ways. Whether they will admit it or not, immigration control was arguably the swing factor for voters in the Brexit referendum.

As of yet, it is not a complex which has really developed in Ireland, unless of course you count the marginalisation of the Travelling community for whatever reason. But when it comes to integrating the so called "new Irish", foreign nationals have mixed well in communities and parishes across the country. Players with non-EU names are appearing on GAA team sheets and virtually no urban school is without a child of eastern European origin. Apart from the controversial direct provision system where asylum seekers are kept in compounds, immigrants to Ireland have not been ghettoised, which in turn has dampened down the sense of fear of jihadisim and radicalisation so prevalent in other European countries. A bus-load of Syrian refugees dressed in the Mayo and Roscommon colours heading to Croke Park for the 2017 All Ireland senior football quarter final is a symbol of this.

There will be opponents but it is a strong argument that integration is a key to quelling hate, disaffection and radicalisation, particularly among impressionable young men of Islamic extraction.

We only have to analyse the events in Manchester, London, Paris and Brussels to understand how radicalisation is the enemy of integration.

Truth be told, I wasn't picking on Rooskey. I could have been standing in a selection of rural towns or villages in any part of the country

IRELAND:
THE LOST YEARS

Rural Towns Feeling The Pinch

I stood along the side of the street. It was coming up to 2.30pm. I began counting slowly: one, two, three ... I reached 45 before the first car passed and there was a sign of life. I was in the beautiful village of Rooskey, which straddles the River Shannon on the Roscommon/Leitrim border. Truth be told, I wasn't picking on Rooskey. I could have been standing in a selection of rural towns or villages in any part of the country.

I had driven through these towns and villages saddened at their demise. I get a sinking feeling when I see family shops and small businesses boarded up because behind every one of those buildings with a "for sale" or "to let" sign rests a tale of financial hardship and a dwindling customer base. There are no happy stories behind those locked-up buildings. And so for some time, I had wanted to stop off and find out what was happening. I chose Rooskey having read a book written by local journalist Paul Healy lamenting the demise of this once-bustling little hamlet.

Despite its beauty and the pride of its local folk, Rooskey is a shell of its former self. What happened? Take any one of the following: a factory shutdown or a bypass or youth emigration, add in a recession and you have enough to put any rural town or village into a life-threatening scenario.

In the case of Rooskey, it's all of the above. The Glanbia-owned bacon plant burned down in 2002. It employed over 500 people from a 50-mile radius. Rooskey was bypassed, having once been on the main road from east to west. And like so much of rural Ireland, it has been ravaged by emigration.

In my two or three hours walking around there chatting to local business people, I didn't spot one person under the age of 40. That is not an exaggeration designed for impact, I simply didn't.

The hotel has closed, the garage is boarded up, ghost estates blot the local scenery and only two or three pubs and one shop remain. And of those surviving businesses, they depend heavily on the good health of farming. This is a part of Ireland where there are not many big dairy or tillage farms. It's an area, like most of the west, sprinkled with relatively small suckler and sheep farms, operated part-time by farmers who have watched their children fly the nest, children who are highly unlikely to return to take on what in days past would have been a viable operation. One farmer I spoke to said that it's hard to know what is going to happen to all of these small farms if there is nobody left locally or within the family to farm them.

And so what is really going to happen to these little towns and villages? Have they come to the end of their natural life? Are we foolish to look through rose-tinted glasses in the belief that the traditional old market towns, with its post office, corner shops, pubs and hardware stores, will undergo some sort of miraculous resurrection? Is tourism enough to keep them alive? And what of the towns and villages so dependent on the farmers' euro, if the local farmer has no one to pass the farm on to?

I drove through another town, this time in Leinster, more recently and stopped off for a coffee. I have decided not to name it because I can only describe it as a dilapidated kip and it would be embarrassing to the people living there. It's a town I used to know for being vibrant and busy but the heart has been sucked out of it and the carcass that remains is nothing short of disgraceful. Big shopping malls and supermarkets on the edges of towns are fine and dandy but they have come at the price of destroying the once-thriving towns dotted all over the country. We are to blame for this change in shopping trends and the boarded-up buildings, dirty facades and smashed windows that have been left behind. Was this not envisaged when planning for retail parks was granted? And what are county councils doing about it?

But what can be done? Are we living in cloud-cuckoo land to cling onto the hope that rural Ireland can be revived to the way it was? There are any amount of pressure organisations, action groups and committees fighting for rural Ireland. Realistically though, where you don't have industry, you don't have population and where you don't have population, well you don't have industry. So rural Ireland is eating itself up. Farming remains the life blood of many towns and villages but farms are getting bigger and farmers getting fewer. That has been the trend for the past half century.

On the bright side, there are many spin off cottage industries popping up. Artisan food products in particular are being produced in some cases from peoples kitchens and then making their way to retail shelves here and abroad. It is not just an Irish problem. It is a European problem, an American problem where there is land abandonment. Luckily Ireland has tourism to keep the more scenic and historical parts of the country in the black. Supporting tourism initiatives and small start-up companies in the food and service industries is the only hope of reinventing rural Ireland.

* * *

Greeks Show Great Resilience In Adversity

My Nana used to say: "There is always someone worse off than yourself." This rang true on a work visit to Athens in May 2014. Like Ireland, Greece had been dealing with austerity for the best part of six years at that stage. My first impression of the ancient city was its visible and palpable sickliness. People were not rooting in bins or lying three deep homeless on the pavement, an image one frustrated taxi driver told me some tourists are surprised not to see, but it was not all rosy in the garden.

We can drive through towns and villages in Ireland and see many boarded-up shops, but in Athens there are entire city centre streets closed down. And they look dirty as graffiti is everywhere. I asked one business-woman if the graffiti was just a part of the Athenian make-up. "No, it's an embarrassment. We just don't have any money to clean it up," she replied.

Graffiti is a non-issue in the overall picture. One in three Greeks was out of work when I was there and two thirds of young people had no jobs. I am sure things haven't changed too much since. Just because it isn't making headlines on the news anymore doesn't mean it has suddenly snapped into a country of prosperity. It once again highlights the power of the media. Out of sight, out of mind. The rise of the radical Syriza party attracted huge media attention as the country teetered on the brink. We all watched on nervously. Now unless you do your own digging, we have no idea what is happening there.

In 2008, when Greece discovered it was bankrupt, mainly due to bad governmental accountancy rather than rogue banking, it immediately implemented swingeing austerity measures which were met with angry demonstrations.

Protests and demonstrations were still plentiful when I was

there, but not as radical. At one demo near Syntagma Square, I spoke to a 29-year-old unemployed engineer. He hadn't worked in 15 months and for the previous three months had had no government support. The equivalent of the Greek dole was €360 a month but it's cut completely after one year, leaving people like him with zero income. His girlfriend helped him financially and his mother fed him, yet like so many his age I spoke to, he remained sanguine in the face of such hopelessness.

At that same demonstration to complain about a new tax on street traders, I was told how a riot broke out the previous evening when 10,000 people turned up to receive free fruit and vegetables being distributed by farmers. Yet one Greek minister was able to tell me with a straight face that their economy was recovering, that the bad times were all in the past. Apart from flying in the face of evidence, such pre-election spin wasn't backed up by statistics. In a much-heralded commentary piece on the Greek economy I recall at the time by journalist Nick Malkoutzis, he documented several statistics, including that "one in four workers don't get paid on time", while 30,000 homes and businesses a month were having their electricity cut due to unpaid bills.

"The social cost of the crisis is often hidden from visitors and casual observers. It lurks behind the sight of apparently relaxed Athenians sipping coffee in the sunshine or seemingly carefree islanders clinking together their second or third glasses of ouzo," he wrote.

I left Greece impressed by the resilience of its people. How some were surviving, I just couldn't believe.

It goes without saying that things are terrible for so many people in Ireland right now, but I cannot help but think my dear nana was so right, "there is always someone worse off than yourself".

*   *   *

New Poor Knocking On The Door

The doorbell rang at 12 o'clock one Sunday. Standing outside the door was a softly spoken young girl. "Would you have any spare clothes which you could donate please?"

"Who is the donation for?" I asked. "It's for my Mom. If you don't have any clothes, would you have any spare change please to help her pay the bills?"

Not that it makes any difference in terms of its sadness, but this wasn't your "typical" beggar. I know that sounds terrible and I have always being hugely sympathetic to anyone who finds themselves in a situation where they have to go knocking on doors for money or food.

The girl told me she was in sixth class. She also told me where she lived and that her mother was waiting for her at the top of the road. I didn't want to pry anymore. I gave her what change I had. She politely thanked me and went off.

For hours afterwards, I couldn't get the image out of my head. I could see the sadness in her eyes. She didn't ask for money straight off. She asked for clothes. And she had her spiel well rehearsed to deal with any follow-up questions.

My own daughter, of a similar age and not too dissimilar in her looks and clothes, was standing in the hallway too. I didn't want either to see each other but they did, making it even harder for the girl at the door to ask for this help.

If you saw this girl walking down the street, she would blend in perfectly as a sprightly, well-dressed 11-year-old. It proves though that you never know what is going on behind closed doors in any home.

When I opened the door that Sunday and saw this red-haired girl in head-to-toe pink with her hands clasped in front of her, the last thing I thought she would be looking for was this sort of help.

Taking it at face value, here was a middle-class family in dire straits. I am adding two and two here, but I have no reason to believe that this was anything other than a desperate action of last resort. A mother having to explain to her young daughter that in order to get fed, she would have to go, knock on a stranger's door and say: "Would you have any spare clothes which you can donate?"

Can you just imagine what went through that child's head when her mother first told her this? Can you imagine what must have gone through her mother's head before she decided that she had no other option but to ask her young daughter to do this?

People might be very quick to point out that I was had, that this was some sort of a scam and that she was taking money under false pretences. Don't worry, I have been faced with those situations too. But I can tell you for sure that what happened that day was for real.

It was a moment in time which, in my mind, summed up the state of the country during the height of the recession.

*   *   *

Hurt By Homeless Man's Sarcasm

As usual, I was late. It was 8.30am and I was rushing to a breakfast press briefing in Dublin's Shelbourne Hotel being hosted by the *Farmers Journal*. As I walked briskly from my car, along St Stephen's Green, I spotted a homeless man slouched against a pole ironically near the old Anglo Irish Bank headquarters. He had a well-worn, empty coffee cup outstretched, and he was begging for money.

On this occasion, bereft of any loose coins and short of time, I kept moving without breaking step. As I passed, he asked: "Can you spare some change for the homeless?" I was dressed in a suit and so probably looked every bit a cocky businessman. I didn't want to stop to say I had no money so I just kept moving, as you do. But then I heard him say loudly and sarcastically in my direction: "Thank you very much, sir. God bless. Have a nice day." In other words, he was saying: "Get lost, you stuck-up git."

I was furious. I hadn't ignored him as such. He wanted some money; I hadn't got it. What was I meant to do? I wanted to go back and confront him despite his desperate situation. I would have told him not to judge others the way I didn't judge him. I don't care why he ended up on the streets. It's none of my business. But he should also know that just because I was wearing a suit and had to rush past without giving him a glance, a salute or a few euro, I wasn't looking down on him. It proves that prejudice cuts both ways.

Why should I be made feel ashamed? It is part of an increasing trend in Ireland: if you are not seen to be on the front line openly in solidarity on any given issue, then the automatic assumption is that you are against it, part of the establishment, on the side of the big guy.

Look online. Every news story invites public comment. We feel pressurised at every turn to show our true colours to everyone else. There are what I would term professional online commentators who seem, judging by their tens of thousands of tweets, to have nothing better to do but make harsh comment in an intimidating tone. And the comment is mostly "against", seldom "for". That is the intimidating part of modern culture, the angry voice, which unless you are part of it, you are made feel somewhat the target of the ire. Even on radio, we all invite texters and tweeters. I am beginning to wonder why? On the one hand it is good to give listeners a chance to air their opinion on something that is being discussed live or to ask a question of an interviewee. But sometimes I wonder if only people with a gripe bother texting or tweeting.

And so here is the question. What is so wrong with employing the wise old mantra of minding your own business and being given the respect for keeping one's counsel?

*There wasn't much
I could do, sitting on the
back of a tractor in the
middle of nowhere,
looking into a field of
cattle and thistles*

Taking A Swipe
At Online Theft

OUT of the blue, my bank called me. They had been spooked and it was lucky for me that they were. I was sitting in a trailer on the back of a tractor on a ranch in Rosario, Argentina, when my phone rang. It was a nice lady from my bank. Once she introduced herself, it dawned on me that she was tracing my movements via my bank card.

After a bit of verbal jostling to try to establish why exactly she was calling, she asked: "Are you using your card right now?"

"Nope," I said, "I am on a farm in Argentina. Why?"

"Well your card is being used to buy items online. Have you used your card in the past 24 hours to buy children's clothing from Abercrombie & Fitch?"

"No," I replied with rising concern in my voice.

And so began a dialogue with the nice woman in the bank back in Dublin, detailing a list of small and miscellaneous transactions which had been ongoing on my card for the whole of the morning.

"Looks like your card has been compromised so we are going to put a block on it right now," she said. By the time she had done that, my card had been compromised to the tune of over €700. I didn't really panic. There wasn't much I could do, sitting on the back of a tractor in the middle of nowhere, looking into a field of cattle and thistles. It would be several hours before I would be back at my hotel, where my wallet and passport were left.

When I arrived back, they hadn't been touched. I was

three days in Argentina at that stage and I remembered that I hadn't actually used my card at all. I had brought some US dollars with me, a currency accepted in this country. So, what had happened? How was my card compromised? To this day I don't know for sure but I have an idea.

I stayed in a hotel in Buenos Aires for the first two nights of my trip. On arrival, like in most hotels, I was asked for my address at reception. And then I am sure that at some stage during my two-day stay, between going to breakfast or down to lunch or out for a stroll, somebody came across my card in my room, took down all of the numbers and then they had an address to match. And that is all you need to buy online. As you know when you are booking a flight, you just need your credit card details and your address and, bingo, you can book what you like.

Lesson learned. Never ever leave your credit card out of sight.

When I got home, the bank had sent out a form for me to complete and have signed in the local Garda station. And the €700 was never actually removed from my account.

We did nothing but give out about banks and bankers during the recession years – and with good reason too. But we tend to lump in the ordinary hard-working front-of-house bank staff who just happen to work there for a living with the greed at the top. The bank staff member who rang me in Argentina was on the ball. So credit where credit is due. And a warning to self to be more careful when it comes to leaving credit cards lying around. Every day is a school day.

But it wasn't the only time. It happened again. I woke up and drew back the curtains. The sky was blue, sun shining. Spring had arrived. It's good to be alive. Then: "Beep – beep." A

China in my hands: Reporting from Tiananmen Square during the 2008 Beijing Olympics

Standing tall: Des Cahill, Gearoid McDonncha and myself on the Great Wall of China during the 2008 Olympic Games. We ended up making a documentary after we got stuck on the wall for several hours due to a thunder storm. We walked around and interviewed other people from several other country's who were visiting that day too

Rio bravo: With Gary and Paul O'Donovan just hours after they won their rowing silver medal in Rio 2016

Silver lining: Interviewing Olympic silver medallist Annalise Murphy after she had won the Olympic silver medal in Rio

Team Ireland: Rio 2016 with Thomas Barr, David Gillick, Scott Evans, Gary O'Donovan and RTÉ colleague Jacqui Hurley. We had just witnessed Usain Bolt win the 200 metres final

Mobile office: Frantically editing al fresco in Rio to meet a deadline back home

Tipp top: Interviewing the McGrath brothers, All-Ireland medallists with Tipperary, during the 2016 National Ploughing Championships in Tullamore

Stateside: With American agricultural broadcaster Trent Loos to co-host an online TV show at the Alltech Symposium in Kentucky, USA in 2013

Makeshift studios: Doing a special report for *Morning Ireland* with farmer Joe Brady, farm advisor Tom Cannon and Pat O'Keeffe of the *Irish Farmers Journal* on Joe's farm in Laragh, Co Cavan (above); in February 2013 I visited the famous farm of Adam Henson, presenter of BBCs *Countryfile* in the Cotswolds near Cheltenham (below right); and reporting from Larne, Co Antrim on the farm of Campbell Tweed during freak weather in March 2014 (bottom left)

Friends in Europe: With fellow management committee members of the European Network of Agricultural Journalists, of which I am secretary, in Brussels 2016

DAMIEN O'REILLY

DACIAN CIO

Above: Moderating an EU conference with then-EU Agricultural Commissioner Dacian Ciolos in Brussels in 2012

Left: I was in Brussels the day of the terrorist attacks in March 2016. Instead of covering a farm conference, I ended up reporting for the news programmes.

JE SUIS BRUXELLES

Shoulder to shoulder: With Ireland rugby coach Joe Schmidt at a fund-raising dinner in Kilkenny in 2015

Down Carlow way: Chatting with John Murphy (right) and a local farmer after John's retirement as mart manager in Tullow

Proud as punch: Tom McGuire, Head of RTÉ Radio 1, with my PPI Radio Award for 2015 Speech Broadcaster of the Year

phone message: "Contact us immediately regarding fraudulent activity on your credit card." Is there no such thing as the perfect day anymore?

At some ungodly hour before sunrise, someone, somewhere on the planet, tried to buy a pair of shoes for the princely sum of €1,763.18 with my credit card number. What were they cobbled with? Gold? A sure contender for the world's dumbest criminal, trying to avoid suspicion by attempting to buy a pair of shoes for the same price as a month's rent in a middle of the road Dublin apartment.

The bank had smelled a rat and stopped the card.

"So, Mr O'Reilly, have you any more questions?"

"Yes, I do. How did this happen?"

The helpful man let out a little chuckle before telling me this is indeed a very common question. He told me that you could be the most careful card user in the world and still be done. So there but for the grace of God go us all, you included, when it comes to using our flexible friend.

I met Banning Garret, a Washington futurologist, at the Teagasc technology 2035 conference a few weeks afterwards. A profoundly interesting man, he was telling me all about driverless cars, food printing, artificial intelligence and so on. And I'm thinking: "Where is all of this going to end?"

Technology is a gift. But Big Brother is watching. I can't use my credit card now to buy a pair of shoes without some alien thousands of miles away trying to do the same for 10 times the price, scamming me with my own money.

That day I had to tear up my credit card and wait for a replacement. Then I walked Howth Head. Back to nature. I resisted the sad futility I often weakly indulge in of informing my hoard of Facebook friends. No, I took a book. Not a Kindle.

I left my phone at home. I brought real currency – no bank cards – to buy my lunch.

And for at least a couple of hours, I just relaxed without half the world knowing where I was and what I was doing and what I was eating while trying to con me of a precious few quid.

* * *

Panic losing hard earned cash.

Yet when it comes to money, be it cards or cash, my stupidity really knows no bounds. I put my hand in my pocket and there it wasn't. Panic! A first world problem maybe, but when you discover that the nice, crisp €50 note you had just retrieved from the ATM five minutes earlier has vanished into thin air, it's not a pleasant feeling. Discovering its sudden disappearance on reaching the till at the top of a long queue in a busy restaurant that doesn't take credit cards doesn't make it any easier. The sighing from the man behind me as I flustered and fumbled in search of money was no help either.

Now, for the first time, I appreciate why women always carry handbags and why they take due care and diligence in placing their change safely and securely in their purses, which are then placed securely into their handbags.

If only "man bags" would catch on like hipster beards have, the male preserve of squeezing scrunched up notes into our jeans pockets would become a thing of the past, and my vulnerability to losing heard-earned cash would be negated. Because it happened before, except that time it was €20. Go on then, call me clumsy.

I blame the small pockets and the law of gravity. Well, anything, but myself. I possess a small, neat wallet, but it was bulging with yet-unclaimed receipts, which are very valuable documents for a journalist on the road. So I tend to go out with my VISA card dangerously and vulnerably slid into my pocket without the protection of a wallet. Some day I'll reach for it and, like the €50, it will be gone too. Because also squeezed into the Irish male jeans pocket are a bunch of keys and the mobile phone. In grabbing to answer my phone with one hand, as I queued balancing a tray of food with the other, the €50 was obviously the collateral and as I plucked my phone from my pocket, it floated to the ground unspotted.

Anyway it is a problem we won't have in a few years as we head towards a cashless society. There are already some supermarkets in parts of Europe that only accept cards. And there are also cafes where you can pay for your Americano with your smartphone. At the rate things are changing technologically, I don't think it will be too long before we will have a cashless economy, whereby we will pay for petrol or the weekly shop with a swipe of the phone. Bring it on I say.

By the way, I wonder how the person who found my €50 note got on spending it.

Yes, I know I am stating the obvious but once the cattle are run onto ships they become a commodity. And it's a €100m commodity putting a floor under a struggling industry

Meanwhile Back At The Ranch

People And Animals Need Looking After

If I were a cattle farmer, I would be horrified to think that animals reared on my farm were being slaughtered inhumanely in dodgy abattoirs abroad. Since live shipping began, there have been intermittent reports of animal cruelty. Even the idea of shipping cattle, no matter how comfortable the conditions, draws the ire of some. So it's nothing new to read reports about cattle shipped from Europe being abused by untrained imbeciles once they reach their final destinations. We've heard it before but we look the other way. That is because this is one boat that can't be rocked at any cost.

The cold, hard truth of the matter is that the live trade is a vital man-marking exercise on the meat factories. The welcoming of a new live shipment by farmers is all to do with economics and nothing else. It is about keeping the pressure on the processors and it's why replacing the live trade with frozen beef is a no-no.

Yes, I know I am stating the obvious but once the cattle are run onto ships they become a commodity. And it's a €100m commodity putting a floor under a struggling industry. As long as the Brexit continues, the pressure will grow to establish even more live markets to Italy, Spain, Turkey, Egypt – it doesn't matter where as long as the cheque from the far end doesn't bounce.

And don't mention animal welfare whatever you do. Hear no evil, see no evil. That is the attitude here. Because whenever a video emerges of cattle being abused, the first reaction in certain quarters is to go on the defensive and dismiss the videographers as cranks, nuisances, sandal-wearing, ne'er-do-well, seed-eating, head-bangers and troublemakers. It is never a reaction of genuine concern or upset – more one of discrediting the story as fake news.

I am pro-farmer. I know Irish farmers take great pride in their work and do their utmost to look after their animals as best they can. They don't want to see calves they hand-reared strung up by the leg to have their throats cut.

Yes, it needs to be made clear, too, that the vast majority of the tens of thousands of Irish cattle travel stress free in comfortable conditions. And no, farmers should not be vilified because they reared their cattle for live shipping in an effort to generate an honest living. Indeed, I'd say all stakeholders here operate the live trade in good faith and under strict regulation. But that shouldn't mean that we down-play animal cruelty just to keep Irish beef processors in check.

Early spring is a busy time on the country's farms. Ewes are lambing and cows calving. On many farms, it results in plenty of sleepless hours as farmers help bring animals into the world. Unfortunately, where there is livestock, there will be dead stock. Losing an animal, be it young or old, is something no farmer wants. Of course, there is a financial loss but it's in a farmer's nature to strive to the end to save a sick animal. Anyone who grew up on a farm will remember the orphan calf or the pet lamb. The pet lamb was a fairly rare commodity on small farms but when it happened it became a love. The laugh of watching the pet lamb playing with the sheepdog is surely not a unique sight to this day. Feeding the pet lamb a bottle or even keeping a sick lamb warm beside the range in the heat of a family kitchen is something anyone from a farming background can remember and still experience down home.

I remember poorly calves under the red light nestled in a pen of straw. And I recall getting up at night to watch or as best I could assist a cow who was in trouble calving. The local vet might have had to have been called no matter the time, the day, the month, the weather.

Before such drama I would have given in to tiredness around midnight as my uncle would sit up patiently until 2, 3 or 4 o'clock waiting on a cow who might need help calving. There were nights I would be asleep when I would get the call in the dark of night to help with a cow in bother. Never do I evoke anything but memories of care and support for a newborn and its exhausted mother. Cynics might call it commerce. I call it natural kindness.

When one animal dies it is never nice, but farmers are pragmatists – at least the loss is outside the door. That sentiment was once voiced by jockey Ruby Walsh. And it landed him in controversy. When asked after the death of star racehorse Our Conor at Cheltenham, he said: "It's sad but horses are animals, outside your back door. Humans are humans. They are inside your back door. You can replace a horse. You can't replace a human being."

Inevitably the remarks attracted a wave of condemnation from animal welfare groups and individuals. In comparison to Ruby's reasonable reaction to the horse fatality, the comments fired in his direction were nothing short of outrageous – and they really went to town when Ruby himself suffered a compound fracture of his arm in a fall at a subsequent race meeting.

Groups and individuals, who devote their lives to promoting animal welfare, including horse rescue volunteers, deserve to be commended and supported. I applaud people who look after abused horses and dogs and I abhor sick individuals who inflict pain and suffering on any animal. But the good name of genuine animal welfare devotees is being tarnished by totally unreasonable fanatics. Any right-thinking person would find it difficult to fault Ruby's contention that you cannot compare a horse with a human. Most Irish people would agree and so you might argue that the extremists who irrationally feel happy to threaten the lives of humans in the name of protecting animals shouldn't be taken seriously, that they should be given a wide berth.

Well, I don't agree. Some of the more extreme animal welfare groups are growing in popularity and are able to call on well-known musicians and actors to back their campaigns. As we move another generation away from the land, young people can be easily influenced by well-polished animal welfare propaganda. People who never stood on a farm in their lives can feel free to lecture the rest of us about the virtues of veganism.

Is it the case that if we stop eating meat tomorrow, they want farm animals to roam free or, have they a welfare friendly cull programme ready to go? Why would we need cattle, pigs and sheep if we are not going to eat them? Why would we breed horses if we are not going to ride them? The question needs to be asked, what other role do we have for such animals in their utopian world?

Be it hard-working farmers or talented people like Ruby Walsh who work alongside and care for animals day and night, they shouldn't have to put up with anonymous threats aimed towards them from behind the cowardly partition of a keyboard.

* * *

The Moral Of Farmaggedon

The definition of a family farm is ambiguous. The European model, or more specifically the Irish model of, say, 60 dairy cows or 20 or 30 sucklers is what we would envisage as being a "family farm" operation, run by one person to support a family. Ireland has roughly 130,000 farmers working about seven million hectares of land.

But in poorer, developing countries, the family farm might consist of one or two animals and an acre of crops. In the USA, Australia, Brazil or New Zealand, the family farm might consist of several thousand acres and several thousand livestock. It makes up about 70% of what the UN considers the family farm. If that was in motor car terms, to me that would mean a family car which ranges from a two-door 1.2 litre engine small car to a 4-litre engine, turbo-charged 4X4.

So, what of the other 30 per cent of farms not considered as "family farms?" Ah, that must be the food produced on the factory farms which are the focus of a recent book provocatively titled "Farmageddon: The True Cost of Cheap Meat". It was written by Peter Lymbery, the CEO of Compassion in World Farming, and it does what it says on the tin.

Lymbery wrote it with Isabel Oakeshott, the political editor of the Sunday Times. As head of Compassion in World Farming, Lymbery came from a certain angle. He spent three years travelling the world visiting family and factory farms. And the insight he gathered allowed him write a book which reinforces the CIWF mantra regarding animal welfare, social justice and the environment.

The scene is set early on with the claim that two thirds of the world's 70 billion farm animals produced each year are now factory farmed. What is the definition of factory farming?

"They [the farm animals] are kept permanently indoors and reared like production machines pushed ever further beyond their natural limits, selectively bred to produce more milk or eggs, or to grow fat enough for slaughter at a younger and younger age. A typical factory-farmed dairy cow is forced to produce so much milk that she is often exhausted and useless by the tender age of five."

It's perhaps the sort of line you'd expect from an animal welfare activist. The book is a dense tome which covers a wide spectrum. It campaigns for the return of arable land to grow crops for humans, claiming that one third of the world's cereal crops are grown to feed animals.

Lymbery yearns for small, mixed-farming enterprises where animals are free to roam. Who doesn't? But have we reached the point of no return when it comes to producing food to feed an increasing population at an affordable price, from small, mixed farms around the countryside?

The bizarre irony is that while not too many livestock farmers would have much in common with CIWF, this book indirectly showcases the family farm system we have in Ireland as being that idyllic model for which Farmageddon longs. When I spoke to him on *Countrywide* around the time of the launch, Mr Lymbery was perhaps unintentionally fulsome in his comments regarding our grass-based system in Ireland.

If anything, the findings in Farmageddon, less the emotion, should back up those who support the idea of paying farmers the Single Farm Payment to keep them on the land. Because it would seem that the alternative to subsistence farming is this factory farming model and if that involves what Farmageddon claims it does in terms of animal welfare, food safety and the environment, then giving Irish farmers €1.3bn a year to keep us away from all that would seem to be money well spent.

*   *   *

The Farmer And The Vegan Should Be Friends

Having interviewed a man by the name of Dr Roger Yates about veganism on *Countrywide* another Saturday morning, it struck me that a vegan and a farmer actually have more in common that they might think.

Vegans are totally against the abuse of farm animals. So are farmers. The Vegan Ireland website has a link to a disturbing video of cattle being abused on a ranch somewhere in the Americas. It's a video which the Irish farm organisations could post on their websites under the heading: "This is what happens when you get rid of farm supports."

The European family farm model is far from ideal – it doesn't provide these households with a full-time income for starters – but it allows consumers to shop for safe, traceable and, dare I say it, cheap food. European farmers draw down just under €60 billion in farm payments from Brussels every year, which accounts for around 38 per cent of the total EU budget. However, Brexit, security, migration and other pressing issues facing the union is indirectly putting pressure on this fund and will most certainly be cut when the next CAP package is rolled out in 2020. But it is a policy which divides. Nevertheless whatever we might think of it – whether it represents value for money- we can also shop happy in the knowledge that the meat we are buying was sourced from cattle that lived a relatively short but happy life, mainly spent outdoors grazing in this country, and that they died with the sort of finality which many humans would prefer than the suffering we unfortunately do and will have to endure.

I understand from a lifestyle, environmental, health and moral point of view why some people chose not to eat meat. It's a perfectly reasonable lifestyle choice to make, not least if you are queasy about the process involved in slaughtering an animal – no matter how painless and humane. I am the world's worst when it comes to blood and guts. I've fainted more times than I can remember when having to give blood. But I have also stood in countless meat factories and watched the slaughtering process. Don't get me wrong, it isn't the nicest way of spending an afternoon but I have never felt uncomfortable in those surrounds, save for one visit to a halal plant in the United Arab Emirates. I remember one hardened meat industry man turning away and saying to me, "now I understand vegetarianism".

However, I did put it to Dr Yates that striving for the practice of farming animals for food to be phased out is a bit like striving for world peace.

The motives are well-meaning but it's fair to say that there are practical questions which the vegan movement must realistically answer if their aspirations can ever be considered realistic goals.

And then they have a little matter of finding the global political consensus. That said, it must be pointed out that they will have been boosted by various warnings which suggests that we might be forced into vegetarianism because of the potential water shortages over the next 40 years, due to the high dependence on water of livestock. We will wait and see on that one.

In the meantime, it might actually serve the vegan animal welfare lobby better to be more practical about protecting the current European system of farming animals, which promotes a lot of what they aspire to in terms of the environment and welfare.

Irish farmers care about their animals. They look after them well. It's not in anyone's interests to do otherwise.

There are legitimate questions from European taxpayers about the farm subsidies and it is a debate which continues ahead of the next reform in 2020 but this is one argument as to why the Common Agricultural Policy is actually a policy which animal welfare activists should appreciate, even as the least worst option in their world. The alternative is one with no rules. While I wouldn't suggest that it's in the Irish farmers' psyche to abuse animals, the destruction of the values associated with the European model of family farming would be devastating with us consumers the biggest losers.

So the IFA could do worse than get on the phone to Dr Roger Yates at Vegan Ireland and ask for their support in the campaign to protect the CAP family farm model as negotiations hot up in Brussels.

They might actually be mutually surprised at how much they have in common.

* * *

Weather A Constant Challenge For Farmers

My former local radio colleague Seamus Duke, a journalist from Roscommon, contacted me one morning wanting to interview me for a special farming supplement his paper was bringing out.

"What is the biggest challenge facing farmers?" he asked. I didn't think twice: "It's the weather, the weather, the weather!"

The previous evening, I had battled my way up the narrow snow-covered country roads to Carncastle, near beautiful Larne, along the east Antrim coastline. I was there to meet local farmer and former Ulster Farmers Union president Campbell Tweed.

It was March 2014 and I met Campbell at his snow-covered farm. He explained how a freak snow storm and severe drifting two weeks earlier had turned his and neighbouring farms into disaster zones. As sheep sought sanctuary from the driving blizzard, drifts developed and buried them alive. Three days later, desperate farmers managed to rescue some of their ewes still alive from under snow.

The tops of their heads were some 15 inches or more below the surface of the snow. How they survived is a bit of a mystery. Many, many more weren't so lucky and it took many weeks before the true losses were realised.

However, despite the stress and trauma, extreme and exhausting working conditions, along with the heavy financial losses and loss of good stock, Campbell remained positive. It's just in the farmer's DNA to react with pragmatism when it comes to emergencies. Farming really is a game of poker, but at least you have some control of your destiny playing poker.

So much of the crises which have torpedoed farming on this island since the turn of the millennium, be they food scares or weather related, have been totally outside the control of farmers. Yet they persist. Campbell and the other farmers are not insured. The lost ewes and lambs are just that – marked off as losses.

Campbell also told me of the dangerous lengths to which farmers go in order to rescue animals. Although farm animals are raised specifically for slaughter, farmers have great affection for their stock outside the financial consideration. He told me of a farmer's wife desperately trying to rescue ewes in a pen, getting out of the shed 20 seconds before the roof collapsed under the pressure of heavy snow.

We also saw that time how farming rises above politics. Sinn Féin's then Minister for Agriculture Michelle O'Neill oversaw the scrambling of an RAF helicopter to drop feed and supplies to cut-off areas while Air Corps helicopter flew across the border to help out after that freak snowfall of March 2014.

There is no shortage to the challenges facing farming. Low prices, high input costs, food scares and securing bank credit are genuine hurdles which farmers must try to clear day after day. But the biggest challenge? Well, that's easy: it always comes back to the weather.

In September 2016, I went to a farm in Galway. The farmer's crop had failed. The poor weather during the harvest had left him with a field of mush. It was his livelihood. It would be like a shopkeeper showing me his shop after a fire. He was one of about 200 farmers along the west coast who had lost their vital crops to the inclement freak weather. Freak because along the east coast, the weather had been fine and it wasn't until I saw the heads on the ground of the corn in his field, smelling the rotten crop, that I could believe it.

A priest in Kerry listening to my interview with the farmer posted me a cheque for €500 to pass on to the man, he had been so taken by his plight. Four years earlier, weather struck again and caused a virtual famine of fodder. It forced farmers to share fodder and co-ops, the department of agriculture and the farming groups to organise shipments of hay and silage from around Europe. Otherwise cattle and sheep would have starved. It was quite a frightening scenario as it was back in 2001 when the country was paralysed by the foot and mouth crisis.

That four month long crisis highlighted many things. Firstly, the importance of farming to this country. Secondly, what farmers think of their animals and thirdly, the collective support of the non farming public for the farming community. We are after all stakeholders in our food industry. We fund it through the Common Agricultural Policy but in return, the cheque in the post acts as a life saver for shops and services dotted across rural Ireland.

* * *

Our Fear Of The Unannounced Inspector

A farmer wakes up one morning to be greeted by a stranger in the yard. An inspector identifies himself. A woman cleaning her little café one evening gets a knock on the window. It's the HSE on behalf of the Food Safety Authority. Now you can imagine the fear in their stomachs as they are introduced to these people?

And I feel for them. You are doing your best. Working hard to earn an honest living. And then – knock, knock. Some "busybody" in a suit carrying a folder invades your home, your privacy, your life, trying to catch you out.

It is only when you travel outside Europe that you appreciate the role of that inspector in the suit carrying the folder, the ID card and wearing the face of an undertaker about to put your loved one overboard.

I have been lucky to have travelled a fair bit and it has opened my eyes with regards to what farmers refer to as "red tape bureaucracy." I don't want to be unfair by singling out any particular country. Because we all have our faults and certainly there are countries I have visited that have dubious traditions in many ways – from human rights to crime and so on – but they also outflank Ireland in many other ways.

However, it is only when you visit countries and cities outside of the EU that you understand what those bureaucrats in Brussels who make the rules are all about-including those with jobs that fall under that ugly heading "health and safety".

But we should be thankful, considering the relative lack of regulation in so many other parts of the world.

You take your life into your own hands crossing the road. You can drive whatever way you wish.

It seems that you can build houses and shops wherever you want. You can get paid about a euro or two an hour. You can sell food in searing heat along the side of the road. Meat hangs within chewing distance of a passing dog or the local sewer rat. You can fish to boil alive. You can trip and break your neck on the unfinished footpath and you can be poisoned by polluted water.

So while we might complain about the busybody inspector ruining our day, it is in our collective interests that these people do their job. We might not like them intruding into our personal lives. But remember, next time you are out for a drink or a bite to eat, you can be relatively assured in the knowledge that a fire officer or health and safety inspector has been in to make sure that the premises and the food that you are eating are unlikely to do you too much harm.

It might help us appreciate that knock at the door or the unannounced appearance in the farmyard a bit more.

*This is what being
a GAA follower is all about:
Hot summer days, long car
journeys, straight knockout
matches, looking out at the
patchwork mown meadows*

Cavan Football

Born a Dub But A Breffni Boy Am I!

"Nothing beats being there". That's the catchphrase once used by the GAA to promote the championship summer. And how true it is. It was July 20, 2013. I was in Celtic Park to see Cavan beat Derry. As the day arrived, I had no notion of trekking all the way northwards, but then at noon Dad piped up: "Let's go to Derry." Sambos ate and tae drank, Dad, myself and with my younger brother Pauric, playing the role of pilot, set off at one o'clock.

As we drove up the M1 with the air conditioning working overtime, I asked myself quietly: "Are we mad in the head?" before quickly concluding in the negative. This is what being a GAA follower is all about: hot summer days, long car journeys, straight knockout matches, looking out at the patchwork mown meadows. It was a real throwback to summers gone by when Cavan's run might have lasted into high summer, travelling to matches in the back of a car full of grown-ups talking football and nothing else.

When we arrived in Monaghan, we had the customary stop-off to stretch the legs. An ice cream was called for before we set off again through Emyvale, Aughnacloy, Omagh, Strabane and then into Derry City. Unsure of where we were going – it had been so long since we were in these parts – the CN registered car in front with three white heads, leathery red necks and royal blue jerseys became our satnav.

The journey had taken just over three hours. Once the car was parked, there is always that moment when you stop and wonder: "Will it be OK there?" A nice local man assured us that despite the fact that all four wheels were up on the footpath, it would be grand.

As we approached the stadium, to the shouts of "hats, flags and headbands" reverberating up the hill, a poor saleswoman was struggling. Her neat rows of chocolate bars were melting under the sweltering heat. Meanwhile, a man hurriedly pulled up in a van, slid open the side doors and, along with what was probably his young son, began yelling: "Get your cold bottle of water here." You would have to admire his entrepreneurship. I'd say he made a killing. The Cavan lads must have been impressed with his cunning to make a quick buck.

The match itself was brilliant. It was probably the best display from a Cavan team I have ever seen. It was end-to-end stuff. The excitement in the stand was unbelievable and when a fantastic Cavan squeezed through after extra time, the relief, if it could have been harnessed as energy, would power the whole of the county for a month.

Cavan has such a marvellous following. The hardcore followers are like a family. If you don't know someone's name, you know the face and on the way back down the hill, the fans chatted away, slapping backs, smiling and basking in the victory like long-lost relations.

Back into the car for the journey home, we got so carried away reliving the game that we ended up in Armagh City when we thought we should soon be arriving into Emyvale. It didn't bother us. That's the difference between winning and losing.

Forget the sunny weather, days like that are what the real Irish summer is all about.

But there have been bad days following the blues too. Many of them. The following February, I'm sitting outside a cafe in

Piazza Bra in beautiful Verona, northern Italy. The church bell is ringing and the magnificent Arena di Verona is right in front of me. It doesn't get any better than this except that I am crocked. I barely made it the 200 yards from my hotel. You see, I have what is commonly known as a bad back. And anyone who has a bad back will sympathise.

Is this a sort of karma I wonder? I complain about people sauntering along the street holding everyone up. It's a pet hate. Well now that's me, shuffling along. It was a Saturday night. So simple. I dropped a euro on the ground in a shop and bent down to pick it up. Click. I knew immediately what had happened. I have had it before. And an MRI showed that I had a bulging disc when this happened this bad last time about five years before.

I will never forget it. One night barely able to move, I suddenly began feeling unwell. So I crawled on all fours up to bed to try to sleep it off. It got worse. It was a bug and I wanted to get sick. I had to use the pillowcase as the sick bag. Then the next time I felt it, I slid onto the floor and crawled into the bathroom and waited to get sick again. But there was nothing there. I had dry retching. As my head was ready to explode, the effort to vomit meant all my muscles were seizing up and the bulging discs were now right on the nerve. It was the worst pain ever, so much so that I bit into the hard wooden toilet seat with my canine tooth which left an incision.

Yes, I had had little twinges and tweaks here and there but nothing as bad as this. And now it was back as I sat in the Verona cafe concerned that a wrong step could cause me immense pain a couple of thousand miles from home.

Picking up the coin a couple of weeks earlier was the cause of this latest pain fest. Initially it wasn't too bad and once I got home and lay down I was fine. I thought that with a bit of heat and rest, the jelly-like disc might just slip back into place.

I had promised to take Patrick to Omagh to see Cavan play Tyrone. His teacher was on the Cavan team. I didn't want to disappoint him as he was looking forward to the journey in a classy car I had been trying out because my own, a bit like myself, was crocked.

When we reached Healy Park, it was sleeting down. I got out of the car and was left momentarily paralysed, grabbling for Patrick with one arm and a wall with the other. My boy had to link me to the stadium – a sad-looking sight. We should have stayed at home. The pain was unreal. I couldn't walk or stand. We eventually made it home. Sitting in the driving position is bad for it but the pain I could handle. Cavan lost by the narrowest of margins. I didn't care, I just wanted to get home and lie down flat on my back. Watching Cavan play football had always been painful, but never this bad!

* * *

Game Called Off – And We're Nearly At The Venue

A little over a year later we left Dublin at half past eleven in the morning on the road to Omagh. It looked as if Storm Ewan had blown himself out. All I was worried about was the storm Mickey Harte might have waiting for us in Healy Park. Twelve months ago, Patrick and I had set off through the snow to the same venue. It was cold, Cavan lost and I tweaked my back which hadn't been right since. Fool me once, and all of that.

That day we were rushing and barely made the throw-in. So we left on time, this time. Stopped in Monaghan for a sandwich and a cuppa. No traffic. No hassle. No stress as we meandered our way across the border. Until my phone beeped just as we passed a sort of Welcome-to-Omagh sign. I threw it over to Patrick, "what is the message?"

"Referee just called the game off."

"Ha, ha, Patrick very funny."

"Look Dad," he exclaimed, pushing the phone back towards me.

I pulled in to read the message for myself and confirm the news of the late postponement with a phone call to a man who should know, my friend Declan Woods from Killeshandra who had just arrived ahead of us along with a fair few car loads from Cavan. It was 1:30 pm, an hour before throw in. The wee man and I looked at each other and laughed as I coloured the air blue with a few choice words. We turned the car and headed for home.

All we could do was laugh. Seriously, on the weekend that the GAA had introduced a "Super 8" competition to make it sound more and more like a professional outfit, they still have a rule which does not allow anyone bar the match referee to call off a game, although I am told any half-wit could have made the call in Omagh at half past 10 that morning, such was the state of the pitch.

Anyway, the last time I fell victim to such an embarrassing fool's errand was back about 25 years previously when Cavan had a middlin' team competing in Division One. We took the train to Killarney for a crack at the mighty Kerry. On arrival hours and hours later, the match was called off. I was on the Club Orange those times as we passed the afternoon in a welcoming local hostelry until the return train home. Arriving at Heuston Station, tired and emotional after a total waste of a day, one merry optimist looking for a way of justifying our calamitous expedition chirped: "At least we can say we weren't bet anyway."

* * *

Meath And Cavan – A Rivalry For The Ages

"Will we go to Navan on Saturday evening?" That's my father's way of saying, "we are going to Navan on Saturday evening". I picked him up just before six o'clock. Patrick wouldn't come with us. Said he wasn't interested. He wanted to watch some soccer match on TV. He had just turned seven the previous Tuesday; maybe with age will come some sense, I thought. I mean why would he not want to go to Páirc Tailteann on a crisp cold and wet March night to watch Meath and Cavan in Division Three of the National League. Like, what child wouldn't crave such a night out?

When I was his age, I went to matches with my father. When the National League matches were always on a Sunday, I would sit into the back of a car after early mass with my father and Connie Lynch. And off we would venture to such hotspots as Cooraclare, Charlestown, Irvinstown, Ballinascreen, Aughrim or Timahoe. For home matches in Breffni Park, we would go via Ballyjamesduff, eat the dinner prepared by my Granny and set off with my uncle Philip and a couple of others packed into the Renault 18.

Of course, being brought up following Cavan would probably be considered a form of child cruelty in other jurisdictions. In time, such cavorting around the country slowly came to a halt. Parenthood and all of that put a stop to my gallop. So having not been to a Cavan match for a while, I looked forward to our trip to Navan that Saturday in March 2013.

Meath and Cavan have one thing in common when it comes to football – a mutual hatred of each other. So this clash had all the ingredients needed to attract a crowd which swelled to well beyond the average for a Division Three tie. Cavan won and won well. They were very good and Meath were very bad. But Meath's poor display didn't occupy the mind of my father too much. Having suffered more heartache following Cavan during his slightly longer time on earth than I, beating Meath of all teams was a tonic, evidenced by the pep in his step as we arrived back at our local St Brigids GAA club in Castleknock afterwards.

Inside, members who took part in our successful Strictly Come Dancing fundraiser two weeks earlier were reliving the video highlights. Among them, the "Strictly" winner Gerry McEntee, the former Meath legend and now St. Brigids stalwart. Having myself had a small walk-on role on the night, Gerry inquired as to my whereabouts for the video showing. "Sorry Gerry, I was in Navan". If looks could kill!

*   *   *

The Magic Of Winning A County Final

St Brigid's in Castleknock, Dublin is my club. Has been always. Born into it. And Gerry was the mastermind in guiding the senior footballers to two senior championships in 2003 and 2011. The one we won in 2011 against neighbours St. Oliver Plunkett's stands out.

Many books and articles have been written over the years about what a club means to a community and unless you are involved, it is probably difficult to appreciate. But put it like this: That Sunday winning the county title was a merging of two great joys in life. The first is watching our favourite team winning a trophy. The second is getting together for a family wedding or some other celebration with your close friends. Blend the two together and you have the magic that is being involved in the local GAA club on a day like that.

At the final whistle, the euphoria was such that we all raced onto the pitch – men, women and children seizing a rare moment of unbridled joy. Watching the manager and my father doing a sort of waltz together is not something you see every day. Players and their families and us, the club members celebrating in unison; everyone on first name terms with each other, hugging and singing as we watched Shane Supple lift the cup.

For such a big club in a sprawling suburb of Dublin, we feel just like the smaller rural clubs. We all know each other well. We played together, we went to school together and we socialised together. The crest on the team jersey is the same crest we had on our school jumpers.

Deirbhile's GAA coach in school that day was on the team so even the younger boys and girls had someone they could go over to and say well done to. Of course, our star man was Barry Cahill, the former Dublin player and All Star. But when it comes to the club, there is no such thing as a star. We all know Barry and his parents and his cousins and uncles and aunts and have done so since Barry first played with St Brigid's at the age of seven.

The texts and Facebook messages flowed and from people who are not necessarily big GAA fans but who appreciated the significance of what this meant to win the county title. It's not just a sporting occasion and that is the point when it comes to the parish team.

"Ye will have a good night in the club," was the customary sign off for many. It's funny the reputation a win like that brings. I blame Eddie Moroney and his immortal words ("There'll be a big night in the Glen") for forging that link between a club title and what inevitably follows at the clubhouse.

*   *   *

GAA-Mad Paddy Joe A Cut Above The Rest

What the GAA means to people I discovered when I found myself at the centre of the universe – Roscommon town.

"Welcome to Roscommon, the best city in the world, the home of heroes and and legends."

That was the greeting local barber, Paddy Joe Burke, met me with as I arrived at his barbering emporium in "midtown Roscommon."

I have had the pleasure of interviewing many famous people over the years but it's often interviews with ordinary people like Paddy Joe that stand out in people's minds.

"That was some character you had on there the other day," people would say. Irish people love radio. And they love hearing stories, accents and characters. My two great friends, John and Jimmy Staunton from Ballyoskill in Co Kilkenny, often spring to mind as epitomizing what Irish people love about radio. A week never goes by without somebody somewhere asking after John and Jimmy or referring to the interview they gave me a few years ago.

Had I been given an hour to interview Donald Trump, I don't think it would have been remembered the way so many people remember the interview with "those two Kilkenny brothers."

Anyway the only downside to this is that they have set the

bar so high that it is difficult to find their likes on a weekly basis. Nobody could trump the honesty, the nostalgia, the simplicity, the warmth and the accents which oozed from that fireside chat with John and Jimmy.

Good characters light up the wireless. And Paddy Joe Burke falls into that category. A fierce proud Roscommon man, Paddy Joe operates out of a small room he has called his barber shop since 1972. And anyone who has had the pleasure of a clipping in Paddy Joe's over the years can testify to the fact that he is a rare character. He cycles the three miles from his home – "the Twomilebush at the Fourmilehouse" – every day. Outside he has five huge flagpoles and every 48 hours, Paddy Joe changes the flags to reflect the different teams participating in any sport of the day. He has literally hundreds of flags from all over the world. As I sat down for a haircut and an interview, the only time I interviewed someone while getting a haircut, Paddy Joe also informed me how he loves his names. "I thank mammy for giving me the name Paddy Joe. I love the double-barrel names and mine was made to be a barber: Paddy Joe the Barber."

He also loves traffic jams. It reminds him of the hot summer days clogged up in a town with the engine overheating as he sat in a car full of Rossie fans going to a match smelling the melting tar. Paddy Joe talked about football, football and more football but you could listen to him all day. In these times of angst when all we hear about is the pain in people's lives, it's rare but soothing to meet a man who has a completely opposite view on things. After an hour in the chair, it was time to go. It virtually doubles as a psychiatrist's chair.

Oh, the haircut? – the longest, the cheapest and the most relaxing I ever got. And if you want to meet Paddy Joe, you will find him easily enough in the "greatest city in the world." C'mon the Rossies!

They are arguably the most mad GAA county in Ireland. I have yet to meet a Rossie that doesn't have a feverish interest in football. It is a great farming county too. But when the Rossies win, we all know about it. Just don't mention the 2017 replay with Mayo. As one Rossie diehard tweeted following their 22-point drubbing in the All Ireland quarter final at Croke Park, "house private, family flowers only".

The man behind the glass had been accidentally locked in while in the toilet. The poor man was from Kilkenny and had just come in for a drink before heading off to cheer on his county in the final

Curious Tale Of A
Man Locked In A Pub

"I'D advise you to call the guards before you open that door," came the warning. The angry man was peering through the glass from inside the pub. My father was on the outside looking in, about to open said door. It was a Sunday evening at about half past five, some time back in the 1970s. Dad was manager of a Dublin city centre bar and it was All-Ireland hurling final day. In those days, the pubs closed for the "holy hour". Dad had locked up at half past two and headed off to Croke Park.

When he arrived back three hours later to open up for the evening, he got some shock. The man behind the glass had been accidentally locked in while in the toilet. The poor man was from Kilkenny and had just come in for a drink before heading off to cheer on his county in the final. Instead, he found himself trying to find his way around a big darkened pub while his seat in the Hogan Stand remained empty.

It was darkened because he had been in the toilet downstairs at the end of a long corridor. It was pitch black and if you didn't know your way around, it would be impossible to easily find the route to the front door. There was an amicable end to that story and no blood spilled.

He told another one of the Corkman who asked if there was any chance Dad could get him a stand ticket for the All-Ireland final in which his beloved Rebels were playing. Dad wrote a letter to the secretary of his home club back in Cavan. Not being a hotbed of hurling, there was no great demand and the club came up trumps, as requested. In the days leading up to the final, there was no sign of the Corkman. Dad went to his place of work only to find that he was on holidays. By Sunday morning, there was still no sign of the Corkman, lumbering Dad with a top-dollar ticket.

At 2pm, he walked out onto O'Connell bridge and sold the ticket on to another man going to the match. When he got back to the pub, here was the Corkman sitting at the counter. Dad politely told him where to go. However, the following weekend back home in Cavan, Dad was at some sort of a function when he got a tap on the shoulder from the club secretary, a nice passive man who asked Dad gently: "How is the black market business going these days?" It turns out the ticket Dad sold on was for a seat beside the club secretary and the parish priest. The fact that he had sold it at face value saved him but Dad, being a law-abiding upstanding citizen, nearly died.

In more recent times, arguably the hottest tickets for an Irish sporting event were for Ireland's Six Nations meeting with England at Croke Park in 2007. My dad had his two premium tickets but, knowing how much my brother wanted to go, he gave the tickets to him and my mother outside the Hogan Stand, telling them that he would watch the game in a local hotel. But he hung around long enough for an official he knew to spot him. Dad hasn't missed a football All Ireland in over 50 years so getting in to a big occasion wasn't new to him.

Someone had found a premium ticket lying on the ground and handed it in. Dad took it graciously and when he got inside, he gave my brother that ticket. My brother delightfully took his seat beside a man who subsequently went berserk. He angrily interrogated my brother as to where he had gotten the ticket. Dad hadn't told Kenneth how he came upon it and this man was wrongly claiming that it had been stolen from his friend outside the ground. Kenneth had no clear answer. If it was Dad who had been sitting there, he would have been able to simply explain how he had come upon the ticket, one of the hottest in town for any sporting event in history up until that point. So you can appreciate the anger of the man, whose friend was probably sitting in yon hotel across the road. For his own safety, Kenneth watched the entire game inside in the lounge. At least he hadn't been locked into a pub.

* * *

Fighting Urge To Like McGregor

It was June 1982. I was nine years old, Kenneth was seven, and it was the middle of the night. Dad woke me up and down the stairs I went. I never remembered being up in the middle of the night before. It was bright outside, which made me tingle with excitement.

We got up to watch a much-hyped world heavyweight fight between Larry Holmes and a guy labelled 'The Great White Hope' – Gerry Cooney. It was one of those landmark sporting events everyone had been talking about because it was going to be aired live here. Holmes won.

Recently I was reminded of that vividly memorable night when Patrick set his alarm clock for 3.55am one Sunday morning to watch Conor McGregor fight in New York. I told him going to bed that, unlike my father back in 1982, I would not be waking him up because I have absolutely no interest in MMA and I certainly don't want him looking at it. I made it clear that he should stay in bed and under no circumstances waste valuable sleeping time on this rubbish, and that no parent should wake their child to watch it.

Well, he got up anyway in spite of me. But by the time he switched it on, it was over. McGregor knocked the living daylights out of the other guy after a couple of minutes. Or so he told me Sunday morning as he tried showing me a rerun on the iPad. I wasn't impressed but apparently it is as common a topic of banter in the schoolyard now as any mainstream sport.

When Holmes fought Cooney, there was so much hype that police snipers were deployed on rooftops around Caesars Palace in Las Vegas, fearing an attack on Holmes by white supremacists, while black groups said they would retaliate with guns if Holmes was popped. No surprise that promoter Don King was front and centre to it all.

Disproportionate hype seems to be the fuel also to this MMA balderdash which has gripped sports fans here and, in particular, young and impressionable boys. Boxing is fine in my book but kicking and punching the lard out of each other in a cage is another thing. I just don't get it. That may seem like a lazy broad-brush stiff-lipped attitude which incenses hardcore MMA fans, but I am not being a prude. I just don't like it. McGregor himself is not behind the door in feeding the hype and buffoonery which precedes every fight but I will say one thing – I admire him. I like him. He has only gotten out of this what he puts in and that is admirable in any human, although Irish people have an unbalanced aversion to swagger and success which I don't.

McGregor has a fairly intriguing story to tell about putting in the work to achieve his goals. I give him immense credit and I don't begrudge him for the manner with which he conducts himself. He talks the talk and walks the walk which would make him a great politician if he ever goes down that road. MMA is probably less painful though.

Political Correctness

A Sobering Take On Good Friday Drinking

Once upon a time every Sunday after mass, we would go into the newsagents to buy the papers and wafered ice-cream. Once last mass was over, the shop would serve the customers on their way home and shut for the day, like all other shops. It was Sunday after all. Sunday clothes. Sunday roast. Maybe a football match or a visit to Granny's or Nana's. Jelly and ice cream! That was the Sunday of my childhood.

I kind of miss those old days, the old curmudgeon that I am. It was a day where we took a breather and did without shops and work. Now the only religious devotion practiced by many on a Sunday is to saunter around the local mega shopping centre.

So I am torn on this plan to allow pubs to open on Good Friday from 2018. And I'm not coming at this from a religious angle at all. To have a day when we don't conform to the routine doesn't have to be tied to religious obedience. Yet at the rate we are going, the Dundrum centre and the likes will be open on Christmas Day soon.

I understand that people need to make a living but it is quite relentless. Like Christmas Day, there was always something nice and quaint about Good Friday – not least due to the fact the local boozer was shut. But that will all change from next year, and Good Friday will be pretty indistinguishable from any other. Happy now, are we?

No more than it's the wish of vegans for us all to give up meat, it is foolish for anti-drink campaigners to believe that prohibition will eventually win out in Ireland.

It's not going to happen, so get over it. We will drink, some moderately, some sensibly, some to excess, and others to the detriment of their health and the wellbeing of their families.

So here is the part of me that concedes to pub openings on Good Friday. If you want to try to control the so-called "drink culture", then we should urge drinkers into pubs and pay the premium for the privilege, rather than in the uncontrolled environment of their homes. I say that because despite the closure of hundreds of pubs across Ireland over the past 20 years, problems related to drink have increased. Cheap drink outside the four walls of the pub is surely the main contributor to that?

Take for example last Holy Thursday, the last one before pubs open on Good Friday, I witnessed scores of shoppers squeezing slabs of drink into their cars like it was going out of fashion. If that means opening Good Friday to save these people from themselves, then so be it. Sad either way.

It is a sensitive subject. Individuals and families have been ruined by drink in this country. There is no arguing with that. And maybe I am biased but the pub is the place to drink, not at home. When I utter that, people argue back that it is too expensive to drink in the pub. To me that is not the point. Or maybe it is the point.

You wouldn't drink as much if you spent in the pub what you spend for drink in the local garage. You would also have to stop drinking at a certain point and you would also get your spirits poured from a measure. And if you want to start a fight or do yourself or someone else harm, you would be ejected. And if you fell asleep, you would be sent home.

You see the point I am trying to make is that rather than trotting out the tired old cliché about "Ireland's relationship with drink" and then proceeding to quantify binge drinking, comparing us to other countries and why we should drink less, why not take a different, braver approach and encourage drinkers to stop drinking at home and instead drink in the pub rather than telling grown-ups to cut down or stop?

It would mean people would drink in most cases, in a more controlled environment and drink less if on a budget usually allotted to the off licence. In my opinion, I find it hard to see how a debate about drinking at home verses drinking in the pub could be won by the former. Yes, that is the view of the son of a publican. But in such an unlikely scenario where advocates concerned about our alcohol consumption levels might actually take on the problem by encouraging "drinkers" to drink in the pub, it also requires publicans and bar staff to up their game.

Closing hours should be brought back to before midnight and publicans who breach the conditions of their licence by serving intoxicated customers should be held more to account.

It would make for a more practical campaign than the current "we are drinking too much" wheeze.

*   *   *

Gun And Games In The USA

Whatever about our "relationship with alcohol", I would say we are still a bit off from being able to buy guns and rifles along with the slabs of beer. Gun control is a big issue in the USA and it focused my mind on a trip to a firing range just outside of Lexington, Kentucky in May 2016. It's a Sunday afternoon. Inside it looks like any retail outlet expect here at this place called S&D they sell firearms. They are stored in cases the way jewellery is displayed in a jeweller's shop.

Rory Harris, a friend of mine who is originally from England, has lived here for a quarter of a century and sometimes drops by to kill an hour or two by firing pistols. He has an ID, which gets him, me and another friend, Maeve Desmond, into the firing range.

Neither Maeve nor I need any ID. Bang, bang, boom. We hear the muffled sound of guns being shot in the firing alley just behind the counter. We are given our pistols, a .45 and a 9mm, boxes of bullets, earmuffs and protective glasses and we are all set. It's like a bowling alley or a golf driving range except the target is a human-shaped poster at the top of the alley.

It's quite petrifying. I have never shot a weapon before and to even have an empty pistol in my hand leaves my heart racing and butterflies in my stomach. To think what we could do with these things. An instructor comes over to show me how to load my lethal weapon. One side of me is a big guy with an assault rifle, bullet cartridges zipping past my ear with each shot. On the other, a boy no older than 10 or 11 is firing under the watchful eye of what seemed like his proud grandparents. All around me, an indoor version of a scene from Saving Private Ryan.

Bang, bang, boom! What if one of the many people here decides they want to go on a killing spree? Well go right ahead because there is literally nothing to stop them unless you are quick and accurate to take them down with your own piece. It is no wonder gun control is a hot subject here.

I begin shooting. The power of the pistol is immense. The sound is deafening. What I am shooting would kill an elephant. In a golf driving range you are done when your bucket of balls is empty. Here it is when your cache of bullets is spent, the floor littered with empty shells. After half an hour, we are done.

Rory wonders what I think. I am torn. I can get the whole thrill thing of firing the gun and now I can say that I know how to load and fire a pistol. But if I put my prudish hat on, what are we firing guns for? And what was a 10-year-old kid doing there?

As we hand back our weapons, the man who had shown me how to load the gun and fire, tells me how simple it is to buy a gun. Spotting the accent he says: "Ah, you are from Ireland, right."

"Yes, have you been?"

"Yes, last year with my church choir."

A choirboy showing me how to fire a gun. Only in America.

* * *

So Who Elected Donald Trump Then?

Six months later it was to become Trump's America.

The fact that I am a little hesitant making the following assertion incongruously backs up my reason for making it. Smug liberals have only themselves to blame for helping elect Donald Trump. So why am I hesitant? Because to dare question radical left liberalism is to run the risk of being accused in the round of being a misogynist, a racist, a sexist and a fascist.

Let me try and explain what I mean before I am destroyed on twitter! Liberal values are good and being a liberal is fine. Embracing equality and fairness for all and protecting and supporting minorities is the centrepiece of the liberal agenda. Who could argue with that? But it has been hijacked by a noisy Twitter-based smugness that does not entertain debate or alternative values. And if it is radical right wing smugness we want to talk about, it doesn't matter, Unreasonable noisy radicalism left or right, it is all the same to me.

But the radical left who work off the notion that if you don't agree with them then you are wrong have, in my opinion, only served to demonstrably mobilise the very people that they want to dismiss and whose beliefs they want to overthrow – the moderate conservative. You just need to analyse the votes cast in the US presidential election and the Brexit referendum to see the demographics that fought back, specifically the rural based older generation more likely to uphold more traditional religious and moral values but are afraid to express for fear of ridicule and abuse.

It's a silenced middle ground, made up evidentially by a more rural, older, conservative-thinking constituency which surely exists here too, who feel they've been abandoned by the establishment in the form of lily-livered politicians who are petrified to be associated with anywhere right of centre, even if that is their ideological base. Nowadays traditional socialist politicians proudly call themselves "left". Traditional conservative politicians are afraid of their lives to call themselves right wing. Instead they'll talk about representing "the squeezed middle". Maybe the mainstream media could be accused of the same lack of conviction.

An example of where this radical, intolerant wing of liberalism showed its total naivety in trying to create a utopian one-track view of the world was evidenced by the clamour of complaints to RTÉ over the most recent appearance by the controversial Katie Hopkins on *The Late Late Show*. Despite the fact that she is a professional attention-seeker, this cohort, so easily offended when it suits, wanted to impose censorship on everybody's behalf for perceived offence. It is as if the great unwashed cannot be trusted to make up their own minds about Katie Hopkins and her ilk. Why not take her on and show her up instead of trying to gag her? Because the smug wing of liberalism doesn't listen. That is the irony, the radical wing of liberalism which does not believe in free speech if they don't agree with it.

Another example came with the pressurising of a Dublin Hotel to call off the launch of a political group with mad policies calling itself the National Party. Later on the day of its launch, I heard Matt Cooper of Today FM interview its president. I listened and concluded all by myself and without interference or influence from Twitter, that the National Party policies were, indeed, mad. It's about time middle-ground or right wing politicians showed some backbone and stopped bowing to political correctness, which has only served to create this political madness.

* * *

Why Ab Fab Star Is So Right, Darling

Absolutely Fabulous actress Jennifer Saunders lamented the fact that the popular TV comedy would not work today because the world has become too politically correct. "People take affront at everything," she remarked.

How right she is.

TV presenter Baz Ashmawy, filling in for Ray D'Arcy on RTÉ radio one day, made a throwback remark when he referred to his partner as his "Mrs". Of course, someone texted in taking umbrage to the reference, unaware – no more than the rest of us – as to whether or not his "Mrs" minds being called his "Mrs". My hunch would be that Baz wouldn't refer to his "Mrs" as the "Mrs" on national radio if she didn't like being called the "Mrs". But, you see, we live in a time where people go out of their way to take offence on behalf of others.

It reminded me of an interesting discussion I had one Christmas with a very articulate and opinionated atheist female friend of mine. She takes outright offence to crucifixes in hospitals but defends the rights of Muslim women to wear the hijab. That's where I think taking offence on behalf of others can become a rather tricky business.

If you ever wanted an example of people going out of their way to be offended, look no further than the origin of "Happy Holidays", a greeting invented to appease sensitivities to the seasonal and almost universal "Happy Christmas". People with a lot of time on their hands, eh?

It got me thinking. If these overtly sensitive sods are upset and offended by being innocently wished a Happy Christmas, what a totally miserable time of the year it must be for them, as Christmas doesn't begin and end with that one greeting.

Let's be clear: I am not referring to run-of-the-mill atheists here. Atheists in the main are very reasonable, sensible, grown-up and tolerant of this Christian celebration, which of course is also a celebration of the winter solstice, which pre-dates Christ. The atheists I know and read of, enjoy a very logical live-and-let-live attitude towards it all which is the way all religious and non-religious people should be of each other in this day and age.

So, who exactly are these people who take offence at the likes of Starbucks using red cups at Christmas? Yes, that's right. People have actually taken offence to being served coffee in red cups which hint at Christmas eventually forcing Starbucks into submission.

Seriously, think about it for a minute. If you take their offence to its logical or illogical conclusion, they must go through agony every December. The lights on the trees must be their idea of strobe lighting. Explaining why Santa Claus, AKA St Nicholas, won't be bringing their children any presents must involve brave ingenuity, because, if they are true to their convictions, then it follows that Santa is a definite no-no. Meanwhile, carol singing must be migraine inducing.

And what about having to decline the invitation to your own office Christmas party without making a fuss? I suppose they could always use the excuse that they have their Christmas shopping to ... oh wait, they couldn't do that either.

How do they explain returning a card or small gift which has popped in the letter box from the thoughtful neighbour or declining the annual free Christmas drink down the local?

Being deprived of all those great Christmas movies is another thing and what if they never miss an episode of Mrs Brown's Boys? Terrible, isn't it? So please, be gentle because this discriminated minority community live among us. And it is already hard enough for them without you carelessly blurting out that great Irish seasonal chat-up line: "Are you all set for the Christmas?" Or maybe they cherry-pick the good parts? No doubt they do, the hypocrites.

God help them, but this time of year must be their idea of hell. Oops, sorry. Got that last sentence all wrong, didn't I?

* * *

Christmas Messages Without Christ!

We have had recent Christmas messages from President Higgins and the former Taoiseach, Enda Kenny, where neither mentioned the birth of Jesus Christ. Maybe they forgot. Maybe it just didn't fit neatly into the message they wanted to give which is fair enough. But if it is a case where they were advised that it would be best not to mention Jesus at Christmas for fear of causing offence, then we have really lost the plot altogether. And it's not fair to say that all non-Catholics, agnostics or atheists are to blame. I know many who couldn't care a damn about holy relics in public. We continue to strive to be an inclusive society but tiptoeing around religious gestures at Christmas turns it into a parody. We've made the classic mistake of collectively compartmentalising church scandals and hierarchal cover-ups and ordinary people's faith into one which has helped in forming a politically correct campaign to gnaw away at a part of rural life which is cherished by so many: the silent majority.

People who go about their business, going to mass at the weekend without ever wishing to inflict their opinions or beliefs on others, but who go for whatever reason, should not be made feel odd or in some indirect way, in concert with the more sinister parts of the Catholic Church or the more risible parts of its history.

* * *

Is 'Up For The Match' On Or Off PC Agenda?

Two things I remember from my first Ploughing Championships in Ferns, County Wexford in 1998 were a cranky car park attendant and forgetting my wellingtons. Since then, I haven't come across any cranky car park attendants and I have always remembered to take my wellies with me!

The Ploughing is an amazing event. It's the only one I know where people don't feel they have gotten their money's worth if they didn't get stuck in a traffic jam or get covered in muck. Both inconveniences are integral parts of the overall package.

Despite the success and popularity of the Ploughing, which includes the once-a-year mainstream media interest in all things farming, no doubt it has its critics. The sight of farmers and rugged rural people wandering aimlessly around the trade stands, as broadcast on the TV news or photographed on the national newspapers, fill some people with a sort of cringing rage. You know the sort of people I am talking about – the ones who hate the church, the Irish language, despise the GAA and tweet about their embarrassment at watching 'Winning Streak' or 'Up For The Match.'

The Saturday night before a recent All Ireland final, I found myself sidetracked into reading some of the online commentators venting fury that RTÉ was still screening 'Up For The Match' using the hash tag #CrimesAgainstTelevision. Obviously the programme wasn't sophisticated enough for them.

Expressing embarrassment at the flag-waving, singing and dancing on a TV programme is not a sign that there is a cultural revolution upon us but it does reflect a palpable unease with this snapshot image of Ireland in the 21st century.

Whether it's TV programmes on RTÉ, the Ploughing Championships, hurling, farmers protesting, Irish dancing or the Angelus bongs at six o'clock, there are certain aspects of Ireland which are as provocative as they are uniquely Irish.

But why do we always need to double-check that we are following the politically correct agenda in practising our culture and against what or whom are the prissy "D4" set measuring us on their cringe-o-meters? Have they never been to other countries with potent cultures of their own, even the ones bordering on the utterly ridiculous?

Over the past 20 years, there are aspects of Irish culture which have disappeared – some for the good, some not so, some happily so – but you get the impression that there are prickly millennials who will stop at nothing in their crusade to change us out of recognition. What or who's other culture do they want us to reflect or be the same as? Surely the premise of any healthy multicultural society is to live and let live and be proud?

There are so many positives to be taken from living in a multicultural democracy but it shouldn't come at a price. Strong evidence lies in the fact that close to a million and a half people tune into watch the All Ireland football final every year and the 250,000 who travel to National Ploughing Championships annually. And most of them probably watch 'Up For The Match' too. "Build a bridge and get over it", to coin a more modern cosmopolitan retort!

* * *

Respect For Those Who Vote 'Yes' And 'No'

Probably the only sour note struck in the aftermath of the marriage referendum result, which I voted in favour of, was the abuse meted out to those who voted 'no' or who had campaigned for a no vote. Instead of celebrating the liberating and history-making result, some campaigners lambasted the people in Roscommon and south Leitrim, for example, who had swung the balance to be the only constituency to vote no.

There were even reports that 'yes' voters and campaigners in the constituency were scolded by fellow 'yes' voters outside of the constituency for not doing enough to deliver the result.

The 'no' side engaged in some scaremongering of their own. It's appalling to read that some young 'yes' campaigners suffered sickening homophobic abuse at doorsteps.

On the 'yes' side, the reaction to anyone who intended voting 'no' for whatever reason was sometimes intolerant. In my area, under the cover of darkness, some went to the trouble of daubing red paint on all of the "no" posters erected hours previously.

Journalist Conor Pope reported on how he had chastised a hooded group whom he came across pulling down 'no' posters from lamp posts. Of course, these incidents may sound harmless when compared to homophobic abuse, but it epitomised how democracy was dismissed by some in the search for equality.

Social media played a huge role in the campaign. Both sides used it to present their message but it was noticeable how those in favour of same-sex marriage were more prominent and industrious and it anecdotally illustrated how the liberal left influencers and campaigners have stolen a march on all other demographics. For example, as I watched the referendum debates on 'The Late Late Show' and 'Claire Byrne Live,' all of the comments using both programmes' preferred hashtag handles were in favour of same-sex marriage while dismissing out of hand any comments made by those promoting a 'no' vote.

So if you were to trust Twitter as being an accurate barometer of broad public opinion as both these TV programmes aired, you would have had to conclude that the referendum was going to be passed by 100 per cent.

It suggests those who were in favour of a 'no' vote, 38 per cent of the electorate, as it turned out, either don't use social media, ignored it or were afraid to post their opinion online. I'd venture the opinion that the latter is probably most likely. Twitter is no place for a snowflake, particularly those of a more right wing bias. This was illustrated by the reluctance of some people who were voting 'yes' to tolerate anybody who happened not to share that view.

Could they not see the irony of this attitude while searching for equality for all?

Local Newspapers Still Play A Part In Irish Life

MÍCHEÁL Ó MUIRCHEARTAIGH tells a story of a newspaper shop in Times Square, New York. Fascinated by the scale and diversity of papers on offer, Mícheál asked the Egyptian owner where he got all the newspapers from. "I sell papers from every country in the world," he proudly proclaimed.

"Do you sell any Irish papers?" Mícheál asked. "Yes. As I said, we sell papers from every country, including Ireland."

"Well, do you sell *The Kerryman*, by any chance?" Without flinching, the Egyptian man fired back: "Would you like the north Kerry or south Kerry edition, sir?"

The story may be tongue-in-cheek but it also underlines how important they have been in the hearts of Irish people for over 100 years. They are sent all over the world, not just to New York. Go to parts of London and you will find the Irish provincial newspaper stands still operating. By the time these newspaper businesses copped on to this niche expat market, it had probably come too late as over the previous 50 of 60 years, mothers all over Ireland would post the paper to their sons, daughters, sisters and brothers in the Bronx, Birmingham, Sydney and Toronto.

Ownership of local papers has changed from a traditionally family run operation to consortium-owned investments. Anecdotally, readers lament that with the ending of family ownership, the soul of these papers largely disappeared.

Having said that, while some Johnny-come-lately titles have come and gone, the older and more renowned provincial titles have remained despite slippages in circulation. The big challenge is advertising and, in the current climate, it is hurting all media types – broadcast and print.

But even in this internet age, the resilience of the local paper is commendable. To younger people, the power and privilege of the local paper could never be overestimated. I remember covering a county council meeting in the 1990s. The meeting was going on and on and on and going nowhere with councillors all looking to have their say on some innocuous matter of little relevance or significance. I got a tap on the shoulder from the county manager the late great Brian Johnston sitting behind me, facing the council chamber.

He handed me a piece of paper to pass onto the local newspaper hack sitting beside me. It read: "Will you ever go home to f..k!" The newspaper reporter smiled and duly packed up his things and headed off. The meeting ended minutes later. The continuing presence of the local radio man made no difference. The man from the local paper was gone so there was little point in the councillors proceeding with any more waffling. I packed up my things and headed out after him. The councillors followed too.

"Courts and sports" are the heartbeat of the local paper. Many of our greatest most-reported-on sports stars will have first seen their names in print in the local paper. And any editor worth their salt will have regularly turned down all sorts of inducements from readers anxious to keep a shaming court appearance out of print.

The ritual of buying the weekly local paper still reigns in most households in rural Ireland. The duration of county council meetings are probably still dictated by the patience of the local newspaper man. And the sales in many out-of-town pockets are probably still determined by the attendance of the local photographer at an underage football match or bingo night. And long may it continue.

The farmyard was a hive of activity by 9am. After some chitchat about football and the impending weather, the silage men would mount their giant machines and race off to the big field over the hill for a day's cutting

Memories Of
Ballyjamesduff

The Sounds Of Summer Farming

Buzzing bees, long warm evenings and the meadows getting
wispy behind the ditches – the silage-making time, a time that
I loved on the farm in Cavan. I would awaken early to the distant
din of Jody Gilsenan's huge Massey Ferguson 165s coming up
the road in convoy. The tractor roaring into the yard under a
clear blue sky announced the beginning of a long and busy day.

One by one, neighbouring farmers John Joe Reilly, Seán
Reilly, Louis Reilly and my cousin Brian Gill would arrive. I
could always tell who was coming up the lane by the noise of
their tractors. Back then, tractors had their own distinctive
personalities!

The postman Jimmy McCabe would zip by on his Honda 50
to say hello while Paddy Reilly (from Ballyjamesduff), who only
had one leg, would click his crutches into the yard via a side
gate from his lower field. Michael Anthony O'Reilly in the next
farm to Paddy's might arrive on his pushbike to lend his moral
support.

The farmyard was a hive of activity by 9am. After some chitchat about football and the impending weather, the silage
men would mount their giant machines and race off to the big
field over the hill for a day's cutting. Back then, nine or 10 acres
would take most of a day to cut. Today, that would be done
before breakfast.

Uncle Philip, Brian, Seán and myself would breast-feed the
grapes (lean against the forks) until the first load zoomed up

the lane. John Joe and Louis assumed their roles as "backer-up man" and "tramper" respectively. The smell of the freshly cut silage wafting through the nostrils acted as the perfect stimulant to get down to work. After a few loads and with the pit taking shape, a first scatter of molasses was applied. Now and again I would sneak over to the barrel to dip my fingers into the sweet molasses, only for others to diplomatically warm me that if I kept at it I would "end up running"! If there was a shower we would huddle inside the empty dry cattle shed.

Louis, who was a well-read wit, would invoke the Wimbledon tennis term "rain stops play". You couldn't better him on anything from sport to pop music. I can still hear him talking about watching Kajagoogoo on *Top Of The Pops*. In the kitchen, the table was pulled out to the middle of the floor. My granny and aunt Maureen prepared a mighty feed for a one o'clock serving. Soup, followed by roast beef, finished with jelly and ice cream and a mug of tea and sweet cake.

At Louis' farm, which was outlying, the feeding took place outside, bales of straw and an old barn door improvising as furniture. By 10pm, the dew had formed and the burning tractor engines were off. The pit was covered and silence descended for the first time since daybreak. Boy, would I sleep that night? The following morning, if we were finished at our house, the roadshow moved to John Joe's, then Seán's, the meitheal in action. They were great days.

* * *

The Smell Of Hay Time
Then there was the baling of the hay. Youthful enthusiasm must

have been the fuel to lugging those awkward rectangular bales around the place. Not a job fondly remembered by others, I'm sure. My uncle used to wonder at my appetite for gathering and building those square bales from field to hay shed.

Funny how we always seem to remember every summer's day being sunny in our youth because when I think back to those 1980s months of June, July and August as a teenager on school holidays, bar one or two wet summers, the sun always did seem to shine high in a deep blue sky.

I'm not sure how many farmers bother with those small bales any more but the process from cutting to turning to baling to gathering to building was one I always enjoyed, particularly if there was a race on at dusk to get the bales under shelter ahead of promised rain. You could call it a sort of pre-gymnasium way of building muscles and fitness, lifting the bales overhead to fire up to someone on a flat-bed trailer latched onto a slow-moving tractor.

Health and safety rules would forbid it now and rightly so, but those jaunts home sitting with a bird's eye view of the countryside on board several storeys of bales bring on a nostalgic smile.

And then the process of carefully building the bales into the hayshed would begin over several days. There was a building method to avoid an avalanche and I can almost smell the dry grass now as I can almost feel the nice pain of the red raw scratched arms, a ringing sweaty T-shirt and sticky hot jeans at the end of a session of bale building. The only part I didn't like was gathering and stacking bales from a field with lots of thistles. Not even the big baler could neutralise those damn thistles.

Today it's all about kale and maize and of course silage with new technology and machinery speeding up the process of harvesting several fold. Older farmers always talk about how much less hardship and drudgery there is today. But sometimes that doesn't make up for the social side which was involved in gathering hay or cutting silage when all the neighbours were around to help out, drinking tea and eating sandwiches al fresco. It took several men to do then what it might take a good contractor and his machine to do today.

I loved those days making hay while the sun shone.